Mary,

I am so thankful our class on Sunday mornings. Thank you so much for your heart and your love for Jesus. You are a treasured part of our church family. My prayer is that this book will be useful for you in your walk with Christ.

Merry Christmas,
Mark
12/22/19

Leviticus:
Learning to be Holy

FIRST EDITION

First Printing: 2019

ISBN   978-1-79479-564-8

Table of Contents

Introduction

To most Christians, the thought of studying Leviticus seems about as exciting as watching paint dry. Unfortunately, most believers don't believe that Leviticus provides teachings relevant to our walk with Christ. Let me give you a quote from a Christian book on Biblical theology about the contents of the book of Leviticus.

> "*Large areas of Hebrew religion, such as animal sacrifice or the veneration of sacred places, require relatively little attention, because they ceased to be important for the religion of the New Testament.*"

Honestly, this is the thought of many Christians. Why would we spend our time studying a book like Leviticus?

Did you know that the first book a Jewish child learns is the book of Leviticus? Did you know that over half of the Talmud (record of rabbinic teachings) is devoted to the book of Leviticus? See, Leviticus stands at the heart of the Torah. It is a book that focuses on how God is to be worshipped. The central theme of the book is **holiness**. As a matter of fact, the word *holy* is found 150 times in the book. Even though the Jews don't worship at a tabernacle anymore, they understand just how important it is to study and know Leviticus. To this day, Leviticus is the foundation of Jewish life. Why? They want to know how to worship God. And they know that, in order to be in His presence, they must be *holy*. Contrast that with Christianity. The Church largely ignores Leviticus because we think it doesn't apply to us. As we walk through Leviticus together, I think you will learn just how important this book is to our walk with Christ.

Burnt Offerings: Renewing a Relationship

We will begin walking through Leviticus together by turning to Leviticus 1. Before we get into our text, understand an important concept that we will see over the course of the next several chapters. There are five types of offerings God instructed His people to make. *Burnt offerings (Chapter 1), Grain offerings (Chapter 2), Peace offerings (Chapter 3), Sin offerings (Chapter 4), Guilt offerings (Chapter 5).* We will spend time looking at each of these in detail. We will begin with **burnt offerings**.

> *Speak to the sons of Israel and say to them, "When any man of you brings an offering to the LORD, you shall bring your offering of animals from the herd or the flock. If his offering is a burnt offering from the herd, he shall offer it, a male without defect; he shall offer it at the doorway of the tent of meeting, that he may be accepted before the LORD."*
> **Leviticus 1:2-3**

So, what exactly is a **burnt offering**? And why is it something that we need to understand as a believer in Jesus Christ? First of all, know that burnt offerings were the most frequent offerings that were given in the Old Testament. Numbers 28 specifies that burnt offerings were to be offered twice a day, every day, as well as on other special holy days. Priests offered burnt offerings at the morning and evening prayer times on behalf of the people. However, there were also *voluntary* burnt offerings that the people could offer at any time. Our text in Leviticus 1 is talking about the voluntary burnt offerings of the people.

Before we address exactly what is a burnt offering, I want to make something else clear. Leviticus 1 is not the first place (or only place) we see a burnt offering in Scripture. **Noah** offered a burnt offering in Genesis 8 after the flood. **Abraham** almost gave Isaac as a burnt offering. In other places, we see **Saul** offer a burnt offering before battle in 1 Samuel 13. **Job** offers a burnt offering in Job 1. There are many other examples but know that understanding this offering is important in understanding many other stories in the Bible.

The purpose of the burnt offering was simple: to *make atonement* for the sin that separated the person from a holy God and to *make a request* for a renewed relationship with Him. It wasn't for a specific sin, rather it was an acknowledgment of the sin nature of the person and a request for general atonement. God *loved* when His people offered a burnt offering to Him. The text calls this type of offering a *soothing aroma to the Lord* (vv. 9, 13, 17). As God smelled the offering, it had a *tranquilizing* effect that was *acceptable* to Him.

Leviticus 1 teachings about three different categories of animals that may be used for the burnt offerings. In verses 3-9, it speaks of using *cattle*. In verses 10-13, it speaks of using *sheep or goats*. In verse 14-17, it speaks of using *birds*. So how would you know which one to use? Well, if you were wealthy, you would offer cattle. That was their most valuable possession. To them, an offering is not an offering if it did not cost them anything! Most people had no way of giving cattle, so they fell into the second category (sheep or goats). The sheep was the most commonly sacrificed animal in Israel's system of worship. So much so, if you go to Israel today, you can stand outside one of the entrances of the Temple in Jerusalem called the Sheep Gate. There was a *massive* market at that time of selling sheep for these offerings. As our text points out, they had to be a male without blemish. *This sounds like Jesus to me.* The last category of sacrifice was birds. This was for the poor. Just so you know, the animals listed here in Leviticus 1 for sacrifice (bull, sheep, goat, dove, pigeon) are the **same** animals listed in Genesis 15 in the covenant ceremony with Abraham.

Now, what happened when an Israelite came to give a burnt offering? What was the process like? The animal would be brought into the entrance (or doorway) of the tent of meeting (v. 3). This is the area between the gate and the altar. Anybody could enter into this area. The area between the altar and the Tabernacle was only for the priests. In the Bible, you would read texts where the priests are "before Yahweh." This is the term used for when they are in the location between the altar and the Tabernacle. It was considered a more holy area. So, the worshipper would place his hand on the head of the animal and slaughter the animal by cutting its throat. After killing the animal, the priest would catch the blood in a bowl and stir it so it would not clot. Then, the priest would throw it against the altar. Next, the worshipper would skin the animal and cut it into pieces. Then, the worshipper washed the intestines and legs of the sacrifice with water. The priest then places the sacrifice on the altar and his job is to make sure it is completely turned to smoke. And as the smoke rises, God says that it becomes a soothing aroma to Him. *Do you see that God's idea all along was to have people assist and lead in worship, but he wants **everyone** to be an active participant, not just pastors and teachers? The priest simply assisted the people in offering their sacrifice. Your pastor's job is **not** to worship God **for** you. His role is to assist you and help point you to the Lord. Are you ready to truly worship Him each time you step foot in church?*

As a parent, **repetition** is important. My wife and I routinely *repeat* instructions to our children. Why is that such a natural tool that parents use? **Because repetition creates emphasis.** As the Whitehead kids hear an instruction repeated, they better *listen well*. We don't repeat ourselves because we like hearing ourselves talk!

Often, God uses repetition in His Word for the same reason. In a moment, we will look at a time in which God *repeated Himself*. But that repetition is not extremely evident in our English Bibles. So, where do we see the repetition? In a span of two verses early in Leviticus 1, we see the *same Hebrew word* repeated **four times**! God is trying to get our attention to that word. Look at these verses again as I point out the repeated word.

> "Speak to the sons of Israel and say to them, 'When any man of you
> **brings (qareb)** an offering to the LORD, you shall **bring (qareb)**

your offering of animals from the herd or the flock. If his offering is
*a burnt offering from the herd, he shall **offer (qareb)** it, a male*
*without defect; he shall **offer (qareb)** it at the doorway of the tent*
of meeting, that he may be accepted before the LORD.' "

What, exactly, does *qareb* mean? It means *to draw near **expecting** a significant result*. First of all, as God's people gave their burnt offering, they **drew near** to Him. Their offering signified their desire to be **close** to Him. But it didn't stop there. As they gave their offering, they **expected** a significant result. They **expected** God to move! They **expected** Him to *forgive* them.

Each Sunday morning, the Church is gathering all over the world to worship the Lord. Thankfully, we no longer need animal burnt offerings. Jesus has already completed the perfect sacrifice for our atonement. He was our perfect lamb. He was the male without blemish. But as we gather, **our very lives** are the **soothing aroma** that has a *tranquilizing* effect on Him (2 Corinthians 2:14-16).

*As we gather to worship, are we drawing near to Him **expecting** Him to move? Do we **expect** a significant result as we gather? Or are we just going through the motions? **God repeated Himself for a reason! He wants us to listen well. As we provide a soothing aroma to Him, we are to eagerly expect Him to move!***

You know, Paul picks up on this idea of a **burnt offering**. In Romans 12:1-2, he says, *"Therefore I urge you, brethren, by the mercies of God, to present your bodies a **living and holy sacrifice**, acceptable to God, which is your spiritual service of worship. And do not be conformed to this world, but be transformed by the renewing of your mind, so that you may prove what the will of God is, that which is good and acceptable and perfect."* Do you understand what he is saying? A burnt offering is what they consider a "**whole**" offering. Every bit of the offering is used up. Paul is saying, in the same way, **all** of us are to be used as a whole offering on God's altar. Does that describe you right now?

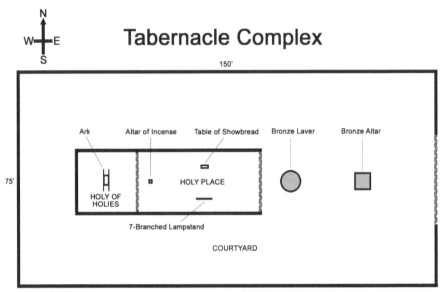

Tabernacle Complex

N
W—E
S

150'

75'

Ark
Altar of Incense
Table of Showbread
Bronze Laver
Bronze Altar

HOLY OF HOLIES

HOLY PLACE

7-Branched Lampstand

COURTYARD

Grain Offerings: A Personalized Offering

Now when anyone presents a grain offering as an offering to the LORD,
Leviticus 2:1a

What were **grain offerings**? The Hebrew word is *minha*. It means *tribute paid to a superior*. This offering was a constant reminder that God is our superior. There is a God, and we ain't Him! Just like a burnt offering, it is a *voluntary* offering. It is not required. However, a *minha* was given publicly at the same time as a burnt offering – every morning and every evening.

So, let's talk about some principles of burnt offerings that are important for us to understand today as a believer in Jesus Christ:

1. **While *burnt* offerings provided <u>atonement for sin</u>, *grain* offerings were an act of <u>worship</u> that acknowledged the <u>Lord's provision</u>.** Grain offerings were often given just after burnt offerings during their times of worship. These offerings were an act of **complete** obedience because there was a great cost associated. Think about it...this was his or her food! The person making the offering was giving the Lord the very thing that sustained life because they *knew* it came from Him. Not only that, it was the **best** they had. It was the *best* of the kernels of wheat. So, every time they gave a grain offering, it was a picture of their **trust** in the Lord.

   *As a believer, can I say that there is a **great cost** in the offerings I give Him? I am not just talking about what I put in the offering plate. Do I give Him my first and best of everything? Does He get the first and best of my time each day? Does He get my best energy? Do I trust Him to provide for me so much that He truly gets the **most** of everything I offer? This is a grain offering. It acknowledges our complete obedience to Him as our Lord.*

2. **Grain offerings were prepared <u>*at home*</u>.** This is such a simple truth, but it is so important. The one giving the grain offering did not prepare it at the Tabernacle. It was prepared at home and brought to the Tabernacle.

   *As a believer, do I expect offerings to only be prepared and given at church? My worship at church should only be the byproduct of what has been prepared **at home**. So, when you go to church, do you go prepared to give Him an offering of great cost to you because of your absolute dependence on Him?*

3. **There was not an <u>*exact recipe*</u> for grain offerings.** There were different ways to make the grain offerings. They could be raw, prepared in an oven, prepared on a griddle, or even boiled (vv. 1, 4, 5, 7). These offerings could be *personalized*. There are four types of grain offerings

mentioned in Leviticus 2. Know that if I am going to bring a voluntary grain offering, it is a very public matter. *Everyone* will be able to see the type of grain offering I am bringing. So, let's remember each type that we talked about that morning:

a. **Verses 1-2** – Some offerings had never touched heat. This represents the scene in life when everything is good. You are healthy. Your family is on the right track. It's not a sin to be ok. There are seasons when everything is going well. In those moments, we make an offering to God recognizing that everything is from Him. This is the hardest place to worship Him.

b. **Verse 4** - Some offerings had fairly light heat. Things are ok here. There might be a bump in the road, but things aren't bad. We are to worship in those moments.

c. **Verse 5** – Some offerings were made on a griddle. There are sometimes in life when you feel a fire underneath you. You aren't ready to call it quits, but you feel a pretty intense heat. Inside you are a mess and you wish the heat would calm down. When we have griddle-hot times in life, we are to bring an offering to Him.

d. **Verse 7** – Some offerings were made from a pan. This is a deep-fried offering. We see great heroes of the faith have moments of being in great despair. People like Abraham and David and Elijah and Jonah and Job and Jeremiah and even Jesus. In those moments, this is where you find their offerings. Have you been here? Have you been to a place where life is so hard that you feel like you are being boiled in oil? If you have ever been in those situations, the last thing you want to do is to sit around people who have everything going well. But, even in these moments, God wants us to bring an offering to Him!

*Do I understand that **other people's offerings** will look **different** than **my offering**? That is okay! We are all going through different things in our life. We have a personal God that asks for personal offerings. Our offerings will not be the same. But know that He **always** wants us to be worshiping Him. It doesn't matter what we are going through. It doesn't matter how hot the heat seems to be. Today, can I say that I am giving Him the offering that He is asking me to give?*

4. **There was *no leaven* or *honey* added to the grain offerings (v. 11).** The offering had to be **pure**. God did not want *leaven* added to the grain offering. *Leaven* almost always symbolizes *sin* in Scripture. He also did not want *honey* added to the grain offering. Why would that be? Well, first of all, honey would break down under heat. But even more than that, honey was a common sacrifice to pagan deities.

*I am to offer Him worship that is **pure**. It is to be exactly how He gives me the recipe with nothing else attached. If it is going to be pure, I better be* *listening closely to His instructions of what He wants from me. I better be in tune with His voice. Am I?*

5. **_Oil_ and _salt_ were absolute musts when offering a grain offering (vv. 1, 4, 5, 7, 13).** So, why *oil*? Oil represents the Holy Spirit. In the OT, priests and kings were anointed with oil. Why did they do that? It showed that God's favor was on them. Do you understand that a grain offering is making the statement that **every** situation comes from the hand of God? Even those deep-fried moments! They were saturated in oil. Nothing happens that isn't sifted through God's hands.

   What about *salt*? Salt is a preservative. In their culture, Arabs and Greeks would always conclude a bond of a covenant by eating salt together. Two times in the Old Testament (Num. 18:19, 2 Chr. 13:5) we see the term "covenant of salt" used. So, salt symbolized the biding power of the covenant. It made a statement that the covenant could never be destroyed by fire or decay. Therefore, putting salt in these offerings is a plea to God to *remember* His covenant with His people. He had told them that **they** would be His people and **He** would be their God. So, if salt is a reminder of the binding power of a covenant, what do you make of **Matthew 5:13**? It says, "*You are the **salt** of the earth; but if the salt has become tasteless, how can it be made salty again? It is no longer good for anything, except to be thrown out and trampled under foot by men.*" When the world looks at you, they should be reminded of God's promises to His people. They should see a covenant sealed with salt. We are to live in such a way that they continuously see a life that is lived for Him. Is that what others see when they look at you? Are you *really* the **salt** of the earth?

6. **While *part* of the grain offering went to _God_, most went to the _priest_ (vv. 3, 10).** Our text says that the *most holy* part went to the priest. It is the *kodesh kodashim*. How often does the Church miss the boat on this one? God's heart is for those He has called to serve Him in full-time ministry to be *cared for.* His heart is for our minister's needs to be met. Of course, part of that includes caring for financial needs. But it is much more than that! As a Church, do we *really* seek to build up and encourage our pastors? Do we *really* seek to be a person who is ready and willing to help them in their ministry?

   *If my pastor does not feel encouraged because of me, I am not doing my job! Part of my grain offering must always include nourishing and caring for my pastor so he can sustain his ministry! Part of my grain offering is to come alongside him and be a **mesharet**. How am I doing with this part of my grain offering?*

Let's sum up grain offerings like this. The next time you take the Lord's Supper, I want you to remember that Jesus became your grain offering. When you take the bread, Jesus says that you are eating His flesh. Why? He is the **bread of life** (John 6:48). The grain offering is said to be a *living sacrifice*. You didn't have to kill an animal to give this offering. What does Paul call us to be? He calls us to be like Jesus. He calls us to be a *living sacrifice (Romans 12)*. He calls us to be a grain offering for the world to see! Do not be conformed to this world! Be *transformed* by the renewing of your mind that you may prove what the will of God is, that which is good and acceptable, and perfect.

Will you be His grain offering?

Peace Offerings: Sharing a Meal with Jesus

Now if his offering is a sacrifice of peace offerings, if he is going to offer out of the herd, whether male or female, he shall offer it without defect before the LORD.
Leviticus 3:1

We have already discussed two *voluntary* offerings - burnt offerings and grain offerings. Today, we will discuss a third *voluntary* offering. It is a **peace offering**. Another name for peace offering used in some translations is a **fellowship offering**. So, what exactly is a **peace offering** or a **fellowship offering**?

First of all, the Hebrew word used for this type of offering is *shelamim*. It means a *sacrifice of well-being*. So, this is an offering that a person would make in times of joy, gladness, gratitude, or relief. Now, what animals may be used in this sacrifice? First of all, it could be from the herd (v. 1-5) or the flock (v. 6). If it were from the flock, it could be sheep (v. 7-11) or goats (v. 12-16). These are the same animals used for burnt offerings, minus the birds. There is another difference, however. These could be *male or female*.

So, let's just imagine we are there in the courtyard of the Tabernacle and someone wants to make this type of peace offering to God. First of all, understand that the person making this offering **always** makes a burnt offering first. You do not give a peace offering by itself. Why? Before **fellowship** with God can happen, there must be **atonement**. The details in offering the peace offering are very similar to how the guilt offering was given. The worshipper brings the animal into the entrance of the courtyard, lays his hand upon its head, slaughters the animal, the priest dashes the blood on all the sides of the altar, then the animal is cut. The difference is that the peace offering is not a **whole** offering. Only part of it is to be put on the altar. You see, the instructions are for the **blood** and the **fatty portions** of the animal to go to God. **Read verses 2-5**. We know about blood. Blood is where life comes from. That is Leviticus 17. So, blood would go to God, not to man. But why the fat? Why the kidneys? Why the liver? Why do those have to be given to God by being burned on the altar? Well, the fatty portions were considered the *richest, tastiest* part of the meal. It would be like if you had a distinguished guest come to your house and you wanted to give that person the best part of the meal you had to offer. But understand that the kidneys and liver have a lot of fat around them. So, they were given to God as well. **Read verse 17**. What belongs to God is *not* to be eaten by humans. So that was God's portion. Some of the meat would go to the priests. We see this in Leviticus 7. The rest of it went to the worshipper.

You have to get this picture. This offering was an offering in which **most** of the sacrifice was eaten by the person making the sacrifice. And there is something else you need to know. If you were going to make a peace offering to God, you invited guests to come along and eat the meal with you "in the Lord's presence."

Here is how the Jews viewed this offering. A person wants to joyfully celebrate the loving-kindness of his God by feasting in God's presence. So, he gets his friends together. He brings his burnt offering sacrifice along with his peace offering sacrifice and heads to the Tabernacle. After offering the burnt offering, it is time to share a meal with God. So, the worshipper transfers the *ownership* of his animal to God. How? By giving God the blood and the fat. The act of giving these things is telling God, "You own this animal." Next, the worshipper eats his portion...but these portions were said to be given back to him **by God**. It's the very same idea as to when a king is sustained by the people that he rules. The people's money is what pays for the food. Yet, how big an honor it is for someone to be invited to the king's house to *dine with him*. This is exactly how a Jew viewed this peace offering. It is God inviting him to dine with Him.

Where do we see peace offerings in the Bible? Well, they are all over the place! In Exodus 24:5, the people were going to seal the covenant with God at Mt. Sinai. So, they had a *peace offering*. In 1 Samuel 11:15, the people are installing Saul as the King of Israel. So, they had a *peace offering*. In 2 Samuel 16:17-18, David is bringing the Ark of the Covenant to Jerusalem. They had a *peace offering*. In 1 Kings 8:64 there is the dedication of Solomon's Temple. They had a *peace offering*.

There were **3 types** of peace offerings. As stated previously, the Hebrew word for peace offerings is *shelamim*. Any Hebrew word that ends with –*im* is plural. **Leviticus 7:11-16** tells us the three types of these offerings. I think it is worth our time looking at these three types.

1. **Praise-thank offering (*tôdâ*)** - This type of peace offering acknowledged God's work as "spot on" in all His dealings with His people. Let's say you were thankful to God for something He did in your life, this would be a time to make this type of *peace offering*.
2. **Vow offering (*nēder*)** - This type of peace offering sealed a pledge to obey what the Lord put in the heart of His people through faith. Let's say God made it clear that He wanted you to help with our youth group. You would have a *peace offering* telling the Lord that you will obey Him.
3. **Free-will offering (*neaba*)** - This type of peace offering expressed full commitment in spontaneous love for the Lord. It focused on simply desiring more of God's fellowship. Have you ever been there? Have you ever just felt an overwhelming love for the Lord and wanted Him to know it? You would have a *peace offering* in these moments.

What was the common theme of all of these peace offerings? No matter the *reason* behind the offering, each one **always** concluded with a holy meal with God. It is as if God threw a party and invited His people to come and dine with Him as His special guests.

You know, even today there is something special about sharing a meal with someone else. Not that we have time today, but I bet some of you have stories about sharing a meal with some pretty amazing people. Sharing a meal is unique because it is what *friends* do. Sharing a meal is what *families* do. I want you to think about the Last Supper. What must it have been like to be a disciple of Jesus and share a meal with Him?

Peace offerings were a chance for God's people to share a meal with Him.

This doesn't mean we need to turn back the clocks and long for the ability to offer *peace offerings* that we see under the old covenant. You see, a day is coming when we will share a meal with our Savior, too!

> *"Let us rejoice and be glad and give the glory to Him, for the marriage of the Lamb has come and His bride has made herself ready." It was given to her to clothe herself in fine linen, bright and clean; for the fine linen is the righteous acts of the saints. Then he said to me, "Write, 'Blessed are those who are invited to the* **marriage supper of the Lamb**.*" And he said to me, "These are true words of God." Revelation 19:7-9*

I so look forward to that day!

But you know what? We don't even have to wait for that day to share a meal with Him. Did you know that the Lord's Supper is a *peace offering*? It's true. 1 Corinthians 11 talks about believers sharing the Lord's Supper when they were together for fellowship. As they took the bread, it was a picture of eating the sacrificial animal. But there is an important difference. Instead of throwing the blood against an altar, what does Jesus tell us to do with the blood? **We** are to drink it. We are to drink the wine that represents His blood. Have you ever thought about how odd that is? In the Old Testament, the people **never** were to touch blood. God never changes. Why did He suddenly make it okay? Well, **He** now lives in us! So, as we take the cup, it is still a statement that the blood belongs to God because *He lives in us*!

I think there are some take-home points that we cannot miss about peace offerings. First of all, I am reminded of Acts 2:42 which says that the early believers *continually* devoted themselves to the apostles' teaching and fellowship, to the breaking of bread and prayer. If there is something special about sharing a meal with others, how often do you have others over to your house to share a meal with them? Peace offerings were special because they were shared *with* God, but don't miss that people would bring their friends and families with them as they shared this meal. If you want to make a difference in the lives of those God has placed in your path, share a meal with them. Honest conversations happen around dinner tables.

The next thing to consider: What if we had **special meals** to mark the same things that God told His people to have peace offerings for? Do you remember the three reasons they were to have them?

1. **Praise-thank offering (*tôdâ*)** – What if you had a special meal that marked the times when you were just thankful to God for what He is doing? You would *never* forget that meal and it would always remind you of His faithfulness!

2. **Vow offering (*nēder*)** – What if you had a special meal that marked times when you knew God gave you an assignment? Maybe a day He made it clear that you were supposed to go on a mission trip? Or, what if you had a special meal on the day you child gets baptized, committing his or her life to the Lord. It is a meal that he or she would never forget, and it would mark a vow that is made to the Lord.

3. **Free-will offering (*neaba*)** – Right now, I know some of you are really growing spiritually. You are hungry. You are wanting *more* and *more* of Jesus. I can hear it in your voices as you talk to me. I can sense it as I am around you. What if you decided to have a special meal that can serve as a reminder to you on days that you aren't as hungry for Him?

Call me crazy, but I think God can still use *meals* to point people to Himself. Honestly, I don't think I view meals the same way He does. Maybe it is time for us to view them through the lens of **peace offerings**.

Sin Offerings: A Covering for Unintentional Sin

"Then the Lord spoke to Moses..." These opening words of Leviticus 4 mark a new section. The last time these words were mentioned was in Leviticus 1:1.

As a review, what were the first three offerings that we have discussed to this point? Burnt offerings, grain offerings, and peace offerings. These offerings were all **voluntary** offerings. They were not something that people were obligated to do. As we enter into the next two chapters, we will discuss two **mandatory** offerings. Leviticus 4 focuses on **sin offerings** while Leviticus 5 talks about **guilt offerings**.

Sin offerings may also be called purification offerings. The Hebrew word for sin used in Leviticus 4:2 is *ḥāṭā'*. The Hebrew word for sin offering is *ḥattā'th.* What exactly does *sin* mean? It means *to miss the mark.* In the Old Testament, there are two categories of sin. There are the sins committed on purpose and there are the sins committed unintentionally. A sin offering was **not** for an intentional sin. Do you realize what happened in the Old Testament if you *intentionally* sinned? Turn to **Numbers 15:30**. There was no forgiveness for sins committed intentionally. You were *cut off* from Israel. Excommunication. Never to see your family or friends again. You had no hope of an income. You were out. It is the very same concept that we see in the New Testament when someone sins against the Holy Spirit.

A sin offering was not for an *intentional* sin, but rather an *unintentional* sin.

> *Speak to the sons of Israel, saying, "If a person sins unintentionally in any of the things which the LORD has commanded not to be done, and commits any of them, if the anointed priest sins so as to bring guilt on the people, then let him offer to the LORD a bull without defect as a sin offering for the sin he has committed."*
> **Leviticus 4:2-3**

Jewish thought is this: *Inadvertent acts are just as harmful as deliberate ones, the need to atone for them just as real, and the desire to do so, once they are realized, greater.*

Sin offerings are given different ways depending on the **person** or **group of people** who unintentionally sin. Let's talk about the first group. What if the **high priest** accidentally sins? We see this addressed in verses 3-12. The problem is that his sin will cause the **entire nation** to become guilty (v. 3). So, this sin must be forgiven. He was to bring a **bull** without defect for his offering. I want you to get into the story. Imagine you are the High Priest. How hard would it be to admit that you had missed the mark? You are the representative of God to the entire nation. The High Priest would have to humble himself and admit that he sinned before making this offering. That sounds a lot like *repentance* to me.

Picture the High Priest. He brings his bull, lays his hands on the bull, and slaughters it. He takes the blood from the animal and sprinkles it **7 times** before the Lord in front of the curtain of the sanctuary (completeness). That is very different than the offerings we have previously discussed. Why do you think he takes it to the curtain? He alone is the one who goes through that curtain to meet with God one day a year (Yom Kipper). His sin needed to be cleansed in every area of the Tabernacle if he was going to approach God. Next, the High Priest was to put blood on the horns of the incense altar. Does anybody remember the purpose of the incense altar from our study of Exodus? The incense symbolized prayers to God. So God wanted the High Priest to put blood on the horns of the incense altar saying, "I accept your prayers." Next, the High Priest was to pour out the rest of the blood on the base of the altar.

Look at **verses 8-10**. Does that sound familiar to anybody? We talked about this last week. The fat of the animal is removed and offered up to God. These are the tastiest, richest part of the animal. It was put on the altar for the Lord.

Look at **verses 11-12**. The hide of the bull, its flesh, head, legs, entrails, refuse is **all** brought to a clean place outside the camp and burned. This is different than the burnt offering. How is it different? It is brought *outside* the camp. Also, the skin is burned. Is there another time when there is a sacrifice burned outside of camp with the skin intact? **Leviticus 16:27**. On the Day of Atonement (Yom Kipper), this same thing happened. Do you think the people understood the *seriousness* of the sin of the High Priest based on what God told them to do?

The next section of our text deals with sin offerings on behalf of the **whole Israelite community**. We see this in verses 13-21. The procedure is essentially the same for this offering as with the High Priest. They also use a bull for the sacrifice. The elders of the community put their head on the bull's head as it is slaughtered. The put it on the veil, the horns of the altar of incense, and pour out the rest at the base of the altar. The fat is removed and burned on the altar. The rest is taken out of the camp and burned. But look at **verse 20**. Did you know this is the first place in the Bible that talks about *forgiveness of sin*? In every case that this word is used in Scripture, God is the One who does the forgiving. It is a picture of having sins *washed away*. That is this Hebrew word. Now, why do you think the scribes reacted the way they did when Jesus announced that the sins of the paralytic had been forgiven in Mark 2:7? Jesus was saying that He was *equal* to God. In their minds, the only one who can forgive sin is God because God is the subject of **every** time this word is used in Scripture. But understand the weight of Leviticus 4:20. God **promised** that their sins would be forgiven by this offering. There would be no further consequences.

So if you were the High Priest or if sin had been committed by the Israelite community, a **bull** was offered. It was the most costly offering they could make.

Our next person mentioned on the sin offering is a **ruler** (verses 22-26). Your Bible may say *leader*. It is actually a *political leader*. What was a ruler to offer as his sin offering? A **male goat**. Now, there are other differences with this offering. Blood is never taken into the Holy Place. They did not put it on the veil or the horns of the incense altar. Instead, they put it on the horns of the altar of burnt offering. Another difference is that the rest of the animal is not taken outside the camp to be burned. Why the difference? Jews have taught ever since this instruction was given to them that the seriousness of sin may differ. If the High Priest sins, that is very serious because it will affect *all* of the people. After all, he is the leader. If it is a political ruler, it is serious but not as serious as the High Priest.

The last group mentioned for the sin offering is that of an **individual** (verses 27-35). An individual does the same thing as a ruler, except he or she would use a different animal for sacrifice. What animal would they use? **A female lamb** (v. 32).

Recall from our teaching on burnt offerings that there was a sliding scale of what animal to offer based on a family's wealth. It is the same idea here with sin offerings, but instead of it being based on wealth, it is based on status. High Priest? Offer a bull. Ruler? Offer a goat. Individual? Offer a lamb. This sounds an awful lot like **James 3:1**. Do you understand that God still says that punishment is more severe for those He has put in charge of others? I *love* teaching. But I better be walking out what I am teaching! This is a warning given way before James 3. There was a warning back in Leviticus 4!

How often do we sin *unintentionally*?

My son, Nolan, is a boy that *loves* to play outside. This time of year, we are at the ballpark a lot. There is one common feature when gets home. He stinks! And he doesn't even know that he stinks! For some reason, he *never* wants to take a shower when he gets home. If it was up to him, he would say that it is totally unnecessary!

Question: What happens when we *unintentionally* sin? Does God hold sin against us if we don't realize that we missed the mark?

See, the Lord prescribed an offering for His people when they sinned *unintentionally*. Why would we need an offering for sin that we don't know about? It is because even our *unintentional sin* separates us from Him.

> *"But your **iniquities** have **made a separation between you and your God**, And your sins have hidden His face from you so that He does not hear." Isaiah 59:2*

Therefore, God had to create a remedy for us. A *sin offering*.

As we have discussed in great detail the way you give a sin offering, it must have been an absolute bloody mess! Can you just imagine the gruesome sight of all that blood on the curtains, horns of the altar, and around the altar?

Was all of that blood really necessary? **Yes!**

> *"And according to the Law, one may almost say, all things are* **cleansed with blood***, and* **without shedding of blood there is no forgiveness***." Hebrews 9:22*

There have been many times in my life when I made a mistake and my response was, "But I didn't mean to." Kind of like Nolan. When he gets home from the ball field, he doesn't *mean* to smell bad. But he *still* needs a shower to wash the stench off.

When it comes to my sin, excuses will never cut it. One day, I will stand before the Lord to give account for **all** my sin...*intentional* **and** *unintentional*. **Without shedding of blood, there is no forgiveness.** So, who will pay for that sin?

Praise our Heavenly Father who provided the ultimate **sin offering** *using the blood of Jesus Christ! Praise Him that we do not need an animal sacrifice to pay for our sins. Praise Him that He has covered* **all** *our sins...even the sins that we don't know about. But how many around us, on that Judgment Day, will be paying for their own sin with their own blood? We must tell the world about the purchase price of blood that has* **already** *been paid on our behalf. We must tell the world about Jesus!*

Guilt Offerings: The Incredible Gift of Restitution

Leviticus 5 discusses the fifth and final offering. The *guilt offering (asham)*, also known as the *trespass offering*, is probably the hardest of the five offerings to understand. It has also been debated more than any other offering. If you open your Bible to Leviticus 5, understand that different translations have different headings at the beginning of the chapter. The New American Standard Bible says "The Law of Guilt Offerings" just before the chapter. Other translations have a heading before the fourteenth verse. Why? Look at **Leviticus 5:5-6**.

So it shall be when he becomes guilty in one of these, that he shall confess that in which he has sinned. He shall also bring his guilt offering to the LORD for his sin which he has committed,
Leviticus 5:5-6a

Some translations say *nothing* about a guilt offering here. However, in the original Hebrew text, a *guilt offering* is mentioned in addition to a sin offering for the four offenses seen in the first four verses. Know that there is a lot of confusion about *guilt offerings*. You see, scholars have debated for years what the difference is between the *sin* offerings and the *guilt* offerings. Let me give you some examples:

1. Philo – The sin offering was presented for involuntary faults against one's neighbor, while the guilt offering covered involuntary faults against God.
2. Josephus – The presence of witnesses was the criterion that separated these two types of sacrifices. The sin offering was brought before witnesses, but the guilt offering was not.
3. Origen – The main difference between the sin offering and the guilt offering is the gravity of the sin committed. The sin offering was offered for offenses that deserved death, while the guilt offering was for less grievous sins.
4. Augustine – The sin offering was presented for sins of commission while guilt offering was for sins of omission.

The point is that guilt offerings have been widely debated. Let's begin by looking at **Leviticus 5:14-19**. We see two instances in which *guilt offerings* were required in these verses. Now, Jews teach that these offerings were *always* given because of a **breach of faith against Yahweh**. Why? Look at how it begins in **Levitcus 5:15**. *"If a person acts **unfaithfully**..."* This word "ma'al" literally means a *breach of faith against Yahweh*. Remember this tidbit because it is important. Let's look at **Leviticus 5:15-16**. In these verses, the guilt offering is given if a person deals faithlessly in matters of the sanctuary. Let's say you are an ordinary person (not a priest) and go to the Tabernacle one day. What if you touch something that was only designated for the priest? See, the Bible says that the things belonging to the Tabernacle/Temple were "most holy." So the bread of the Presence, the incense, and the Tent of Meeting were all "most holy." There were also "holy" things located there. Things such as tithes, first fruits, and anything else donated to

Yahweh. If a layman *took* or even *touched* these things, it was considered a *breach of faith against Yahweh*. He would need to make a guilt offering. He would bring a ram without defect. Notice that it had to be of a certain value (verse 15). And then add 1/5th to it (verse 16). We will talk in more detail about how it is given in a moment.

Now, look at **verses 17-18**. In these verses, a person breaks one of Yahweh's commandments without knowing it. These two verses are very unclear, but rabbis teach that this is talking about a person that just has the weight of sin on his shoulders and he isn't sure what sin he has committed. In this case, he would bring a *guilt offering*. If the sin was eventually realized, he would still bring a *sin offering* for that sin at some point. But the *guilt offering* would be given in the meantime.

In **Leviticus 6:1-7**, we see yet another example of when a *guilt offering* is to be given. Look at **verse 2**. It says something very similar to what we discussed earlier. *"When a person sins and acts **unfaithfully** against the Lord."* What did we say that word meant? "ma'al" – a *breach of faith against Yahweh*. But then it goes on and discusses four ways this happens. By *deceiving* someone, by *robbing* someone, by *extorting* someone, or by *finding something someone lost and lying about it*. Let me ask you a question. In these instances, how is this a breach of faith against Yahweh? It seems to me that it is more of a breach of faith against another person. Well, the answer is only found if we understand their culture. If someone is suspected of deceiving, robbing, or extorting someone, they were to take a *solemn oath of innocence*. They believed if they lied under this oath, God would activate the curse implied by the oath. So, if they lied under this oath, they are swearing falsely in God's name.

So, how did this work? Imagine living before the time of Christ in Israel. Let's say you are having a hard time making ends meet and steal $100 from another person. Under the Law, you would first have to **confess** your sin and then you would be required to repay the $100 *plus* 20% to the person you stole money from. So, you would pay them $120. After this, you would make a blood sacrifice (*guilt offering*) which did two things: reconciled you with the person you offended **and** reconciled you with God. We see this idea in Jesus' teaching in **Matthew 5:23-24**. God essentially says, "Don't make an offering to me unless you have made things right with *each other*." I don't know that we always take this seriously. But before we can be *reconciled with God*, we have to be *reconciled with each other*. This is also found in the guilt offering. Restitution always accompanies genuine repentance.

What about the guilt offering itself? How did this work? We see the details listed in Leviticus 7. A ram was to be slaughtered in the same place as the burnt offering. Its blood was thrown against all sides of the altar. Its fat, kidneys, and liver were burned on the altar.

The issue with the guilt offering is that **God's Name** is at stake. In each of these cases, His reputation is on the line because His people are supposed to look and act like Him. We are His representatives.

We have two options in everything we do – we can **hallow the name** (*Kiddush Hashem*) or we can **profane the name** (*Hillul Hashem*). These phrases are everywhere in Jewish literature. Let me give you an illustration of what it means to *hallow the name (Kiddush Hashem).* About a hundred years before Jesus, there was a Jewish sage named Simeon ben Shetach. One day his disciples bought their rabbi a donkey from a wealthy Arab trader. Simeon was poor and they thought this donkey wound ease his daily burdens. As they combed through the mane of the donkey, they found a jewel that had fallen from an expensive load carried by the Arab trader. The disciples rejoiced. Their rabbi had newfound wealth! But Simeon refused it. He ordered his disciples to return the jewel to the Arab. When they found him, the Arab was amazed. He said, "*Blessed be the God of Simeon ben Shetach.*" This is **Kiddush Hashem**. It means that we live in such a way as to bring glory to God among those who do not know Him. The idea is to associate loving deeds with the reputation of God.

Contrast this with the idea of *Hillul Hashem* (to **profane** the name). In 2009, Nidal Hasan opened fire on a crowd of soldiers preparing for deployment in Fort Hood, TX and killed 13 people. As he opened fire, he yelled, "*Allahu Akbar*" which means "Allah is great." Do you think that act brought *glory* to Allah? Did people think *more* of Allah than before committing this act? No. It's quite the opposite. The world wonders, "What kind of wicked god do you serve who commands you do such terrible things?" But this doesn't just happen with mass shootings. We can *profane* God's name by not representing Him well. We can *profane* His name by not being honest with those around us. We can *profane* His name by point people *away* from Christ rather than *towards* Christ. Look at **1 John 4:20**. Is there someone you have something against right now? God sees it as an *offense toward Him* when we don't love others. Why? We are *profaning* His name. *Hillul Hashem.*

The Lord's prayer begins by saying, "Our Father who is in Heaven, **hallowed** be Your name." Our role as believers is to continuously live lives that *hallow* the name of Jesus. We are to make much of Him and always bring glory to Him.

One final thought on guilt offerings. Even today, God desires *restitution* with His people when we fail. The moment we are saved, we become **his child**. We are *adopted* and become *co-heirs* with Jesus. Just like my children will *always* be in my family no matter what they do, my **relationship** with God will never change. I AM HIS CHILD! The problem is that **sin** affects our **fellowship** with Him. We have talked about this idea previously. When we have sin in our lives, we don't *want* to be in constant communication with our Heavenly Father because we *know* we are missing the mark! **This is why He so desperately wants restitution. He wants a close fellowship with His children!** Therefore, *He* provided the *guilt offering* for us.

> *"But the LORD was pleased To crush Him, putting Him to grief; If He would render **Himself** as a **guilt offering**,"* Isaiah 53:10

Jesus was **crushed** as a **guilt offering** for you and me. His blood satisfied and fulfilled the Law given. We no longer have to live with a strained fellowship with our Heavenly Father due to our sin. I stand in awe that my God would rather crush His Son than have a strained relationship with me...but it is absolutely true!

May we always remember that the price has been paid – we are free to **fellowship** with God as much as we would like. The guilt offering has been paid. But always remember that you have a mission. You are to *hallow His name (Kiddush Hashem)*. Wherever you go and whatever you do, make much of Jesus. If there is something between you and someone else, please reach out to them and make things right. It is time for *reconciliation* among His people so that His name may be exalted!

Chapter 6

The Torchbearer

Fire shall be kept burning continually on the altar; it is not to go out.
Leviticus 6:13

The official symbol of the University of Tennessee is the Volunteer statue, more commonly known as the Torchbearer. The Torchbearer has been the official symbol of the University since 1932. The actual statue located in Central Park was not created until 1968. In his right hand, the Torchbearer holds a torch with a natural-gas flame that burns *continually*. During my years at UT, I never witnessed the torch extinguished.

In the tabernacle, the priests were given an awesome responsibility. It was their job to **tend the fire** used for the sacrifices and to **keep the fire burning constantly**. *As a follower of Jesus, we need to understand the importance of these actions since we are **priests** (1 Peter 2:5-9).*

Tending the Fire

> "and he shall **take up the ashes** to which the fire reduces the burnt offering on the altar and place them beside the altar. Then he shall take off his garments and put on other garments, and **carry the ashes outside the camp to a clean place**." Leviticus 6:10b-11

I remember the days when Julie and I had a charcoal grill. Many people love the taste of food from a charcoal grill, but it also took more time and energy. The issue with using charcoal is that you must *tend* to the fire. Part of that process involves **removing ashes** from the grill. Ashes are the residue that *will not burn* in the fire. Ashes do *not* provide the smoke to ascend upward to the Lord giving Him the soothing aroma that He desires.

The priest had to **remove** the ashes and carry them *outside the camp*. It was a constant process of removing that which does not burn. *As a priest today, I must constantly examine my life for ashes. What are those things in my life that are hindering my worship? What are those things in my life that keep my flame from burning brightly?* **As His priest, I must remove those things from my life.**

Keeping the Fire Burning

> "The fire on the altar shall be **kept burning** on it. It shall **not** go out, but the priest shall burn wood on it every morning; and he shall lay out the burnt offering on it, and offer up in smoke the fat

> *portions of the peace offerings on it. Fire shall be **kept burning continually** on the altar; it is **not** to go out." Leviticus 6:12-13*

Just after my sophomore year of high school, my youth group went on a mission trip to Mountain T.O.P. in the Cumberland Mountains of East Tennessee. During the day, we would help with construction and repair work in various locations around our camp. But the thing that made an impact on me came in the evenings as we worshiped together. Oh, those were some special nights. I remember that week being one of the first times I was truly **on fire** for Jesus. Slowly, that fire faded as I returned to my hometown.

Just as God wanted a constant fire in His tabernacle, He also wants a **constant** fire from His children today. He is not interested in a small flame on a Sunday morning or a flicker of light from a youth camp. He wants a burning fire *all the time. As a priest today, I must make sure the flame is burning constantly. In Romans 12:11, I am told to be "fervent in spirit." Translation: **I am to be on fire for Him! Constantly!***

How am I doing with my priestly duties? Am I tending the fire? Is it constantly burning?

Chapter 7

Being Thankful in Hard Times

You know, sometimes it is easy to tend the fires when things are going *well*. What about times when they aren't? This past week, one of our friends found out she has a mass in her brain. She is in a holding pattern awaiting more tests to find out more information about it. In Leviticus 7, we reach something that we discussed previously. We see the three types of **peace offerings**. Do you remember these?

1. **Praise-thank offering (*tôdâ*)** - This type of peace offering acknowledged God's work as "spot on" in all His dealings with His people. Let's say you were thankful to God for something He did in your life, this would be a time to make this type of *peace offering*.
2. **Vow offering (*nēder*)** - This type of peace offering sealed a pledge to obey what the Lord put in the heart of His people through faith. Let's say God made it clear that He wanted you to help with our youth group. You would have a *peace offering* telling the Lord that you will obey Him.
3. **Free-will offering (*neaba*)** - This type of peace offering expressed full commitment in spontaneous love for the Lord. It focused on simply desiring more of God's fellowship. Have you ever been there? Have you ever just felt an overwhelming love for the Lord and wanted Him to know it? You would have a *peace offering* in these moments.

We are going to focus on the **praise-thank offering. Read Leviticus 7:11-15.**

There are times in life when it seems hard, if not impossible, to be **thankful**. I am guessing when someone finds out that a mass is in their brain, *thankfulness* is **not** always the first reaction.

In Leviticus 7, God commanded His people to give a sacrifice of **thankful peace offerings** (*tôdâ*). This was a *praise-thank offering that acknowledged the Lord's dealings were always "spot on,"* **even in the most difficult times**. Through these thankful peace offerings, the Lord was teaching His people that **every** circumstance in life falls under His perfect providence. Therefore, in **everything**, He teaches us to **give thanks**.

> "*pray without ceasing; in* **everything give thanks**; *for this is God's will for you in Christ Jesus."* 1 Thessalonians 5:17-18

You see, before the foundation of the world, God knew that our friend and her family would be delivered the news that she had a mass in her brain on the day she was given the news. It did not catch God by surprise. Thankfully, He is *always* with us. Even when we get news that isn't easy to hear, He is there. Now, I am not God and I have *no idea* what He has planned with our friend and this mass. But I am thankful that He *does* have a plan. A perfect plan. A plan that is far greater than any of us could ever imagine. Therefore, even in the hard times, He teaches us to be *thankful*, just as He taught the Israelites years ago.

> *"Through Him then, let us **continually offer up a sacrifice of praise to God**, that is, the fruit of lips that give thanks to His name." Hebrews 13:15*

We are to give Him **praise**. We are to give Him **thanks**. His plans are always "spot on," even when we don't understand them! And, remember, this offering was always *shared* with God. It was a holy meal that you eat together. So, when you get news that you aren't expecting, share a meal with the Lord. As you eat, may it be a reminder that His ways are *perfect*. What He does in your life is always "spot on."

Allowing Him to Use Us

In Exodus 28, God told Moses that Aaron and his sons were to become His priests. In Exodus 29, God gave Moses specific instructions as he consecrated Aaron and his sons into the priesthood. Leviticus 8 is the fulfillment of these instructions. Scholars believe God gave Moses the instructions of Exodus 29 many months before the completion of Leviticus 8. As we read, the ceremony was to consist of **five** elements. Let's look at each individually:

1. **Clothing** – The priests were clothed for the first time in their garments required to perform their services (vv. 7-9, 13). When a person looked at a priest, he knew he was a priest. Why? Because he *clothed* himself in priestly garments. What are we to clothe ourselves in according to the New Testament? According to **Galatians 3:26-28** and **Romans 13:14**, We are to *clothe ourselves in Jesus Christ*! The Greek word used in these texts (*kýrios*) brings out the massive truth that Jesus has all ownership rights over each of us. Paul is saying, "**Jesus is your authority, your master, and your Lord. He has _absolute_ ownership over you.**" Just as Aaron and his sons wore specific garments to separate themselves as priests, we are to actively *put on* Christ daily. A a *priest* of God, are you clothed in Christ?

2. **Offering** – The priests presented a burnt offering (vv. 18-21). Back in Leviticus 1, we discussed burnt offerings in great detail. Recall that the *worshipper* presented the offering and was the one that actually slaughtered the animal while the priest put the blood around the altar. Many translations do not accurately depict verses 18 and 19 of Leviticus 8. Take a look at the text. Who is the worshipper and who is the priest based on who slaughtered the animal and who sprinkled the blood? The text literally says "*Then he presented the ram of the burnt offering, and Aaron and his sons laid their hands on the head of the ram. He slaughtered it and Moses sprinkled the blood around on the altar.*" **Aaron** slaughtered the animal and **Moses** sprinkled the blood. The worshipper was **Aaron**. The role of the priest was played by **Moses** during this ceremony. If you remember from our lesson on burnt offerings, God was **always** expected to show up and act! As a *priest* of God, what are you offering Him? In addition, do you go to church on Sundays with the *expectation* that God is going to show up and move?

3. **Consecration** – The blood of a ram of the offering was applied to the priests' bodies (vv. 22-24a). This is the central feature of the priestly induction ceremony. It is the **ordination**. Where did Moses put some of the blood of the sacrifice in these verses? On both Aaron and his son's **right ear**, **right thumb**, and **right big toe**. Why these locations? Since recorded history, Jews have taught that these body parts meant God wanted every inch of His priests consecrated. The **ear** was to be consecrated for two reasons. First, it was part of the head, so their

thoughts were to be focused on the Lord. Second, the ear was to be in tune with His voice as he led them. The **thumb** was to be consecrated so that their actions would match the Lord's instructions. Their **toe** was to be consecrated so that their walk would always match His and they would go as the Lord led them. Years later, the Essenes developed a practice of *mikveh* just before the time of Jesus. *Mikveh* was a form of baptism. It had to be full immersion because it had to cover a person's **head**, **heart**, **hands**, and **feet**. The head was to be immersed so that his thoughts would always focus on God. His heart was to be immersed so that his will would match God's. His hands would be immersed so that his actions would be in response to God's instructions. His feet would be immersed so that his walk would be in-step with the Lord's. These Essenes based *mikveh* on God's instructions to Moses in Leviticus 8. See, these priests were *consecrated* by having blood placed on specific places. The times may be different now, but God still calls us to have a life in which our *thoughts* are on him, our *ear* is in tune with His voice, our *hands* are busy doing what He instructs us to do, and our *feet* are busy going where He leads us. As a *priest* of God, are you "all in" to His calling?

4. **Filling the hands** – The priests received their allotted share of the sacrifice for the first time. They presented the Lord His portion (vv. 26-29) and ate the remaining portion (v. 31). The word that is translated as *ordination offering* in our text literally means "to fill the hands." Moses took the fat of the animal used in the sacrifice and combined it with some unleavened bread. Then, he gave it to Aaron and his sons. They offered it is a **wave offering**. We will discuss this offering in great detail when we get to Leviticus 14, but for now just know that a wave offering *always* declared that the person waving the offering *completely depended on God*. Do you see this picture? As part of this ceremony, Aaron and his sons are telling the Lord that they cannot do this without Him. They are declaring their dependence on Him. They need His strength. They need His guidance. They need His wisdom. They need *Him*. That is the "filling of the hands." As a *priest* of God, do you come with full hands? Did you offer Him a wave offering today to declare to Him that you can't do it without Him? Did you tell Him that you can't be the man or woman He has called you to be without His strength, His guidance, His wisdom? Did you tell Him that you can't be all that He created you to be without Him? That is what it truly means to have full hands. It means that you are dependent on the Lord.

5. **Anointment** – The priests were anointed with the sacred oil, infusing them with holiness (vv. 12, 30) and then they remained in the Tabernacle for seven days (vv. 31-36). Why did they anoint priests and kings on the head with oil? It was a picture that says that the Holy Spirit will empower this person to do service for Him. What event marked the beginning of Jesus' ministry? He was baptized and the *Spirit* came down like a dove. There is always an *anointing* at the beginning of a new

ministry. Therefore, priests were anointed with oil as part of this ceremony. In verse 33, we read that Moses will *ordain* the priests for seven days. All of the things we discussed in verses 22-29 were repeated daily (six more times). Don't miss how amazing it is that **Aaron** went from being the chief sinner to the chief mediator for the people of God. Do you remember what Aaron did way back in Exodus 32? While Moses was on Mt. Sinai talking with God, **Aaron** instructed the people to make a golden calf at the base of the mountain! And now Aaron is becoming a priest for God. This is how amazing God's grace really is! I don't care what you have done, God still looks at you and says I want **you** to be My priest. I want to use **you** to show the world who I am. That is incredible!

Now, I want you to look at the very last verse of Leviticus 8. I am confident that you would say that you want to be used by God. But, how does it happen? Let's look at one last thing today.

Thus Aaron and his sons did all the things which the LORD had commanded through Moses.
Leviticus 8:36

Our family has a new member named Knox. He is a Golden Cocker Retriever. One night last week, I came home from work. Knox was on his leash and I decided I wanted to let Knox roam free for a little while. As is his custom, Nolan was busy shooting basketball in the hallway. I looked at him and said, "Nolan, will you go upstairs and close the gait for me?" Immediately (somewhat surprisingly), Nolan headed upstairs to close the gait so that Knox couldn't get up to the kids' rooms.

In Leviticus 8, God used **Moses** to consecrate Aaron and his sons, getting them *ready* for their priestly service. There is a phrase repeated multiple times in this chapter: "**just as the Lord had commanded Moses.**" We see this phrase in verses 4, 9, 13, 17, 21, 29, and 31.

The first step in being used by God is **listening** to our Heavenly Father's voice. Moses knew *exactly* what the Lord commanded Him to do because He was actively listening to His voice! What is the Biblical word for *listening* to the Lord? **Faith**. Remember Romans 10:17? "So **faith** comes through **hearing**, and **hearing** by the **word of Christ**." Faith quite literally is when our ears are actively listening to the Lord's preferred will! I don't know about you, but I would love if the phrase used about Moses could be used about me. *"Just as the Lord had commanded Mark."* Could it be used for you? The only way it could be is if you are diligently listening to His voice!

Another thing about Moses was that he was **ready to respond** when called upon. It did not just stop with *listening* to God's voice. He responded! He put *action* to his instructions. What is the Biblical word for this? **Belief**. *Faith* is hearing God's preferred will; *belief* is walking it out. *How often do we hear the Lord's voice but* *don't put His instructions into action? If we are going to be His hands and feet in this world, we must be ready to move and carry out His instructions.*

As small as it may seem, Nolan went to close the gait for me because **he heard his Daddy's voice** and **he was *ready* to respond**. *The same must be true in each of our lives.*

One final thought. Aaron and his sons "*did **all** the things which the LORD had commanded **through Moses**.*" The **obedience** of Aaron and his sons happened as Moses was **obedient** to pass on the Lord's instructions! ***My** obedience is not **only** for my sake! It is for my kids' sake. It is for my disciples' sake. It is for the sake of everyone around me.*

The Lord will use us to speak truth into those around us if we are listening to His voice and if we are ready to respond to His instructions.

Do I understand the weight of my responsibility? If I am not obedient, the consequences reach much farther than just myself!

A few challenges from Leviticus 8. **Clothe** yourself in Jesus, allowing Him to have absolute ownership rights over you. Bring Him **offerings** but *expect* Him to act. Be **consecrated** with your *thoughts* on Him, your *hands* ready to do what He tells you, and your *feet* ready to follow Him. Have **full hands**, filled with a wave offering declaring your complete dependence to the Lord. Allow the **anointing** of the Holy Spirit to be displayed in your life.

Know that the Lord is going to be speaking to you as you continue your daily life. Keep your ears **open** to His voice. Be **ready to respond** as He reveals Himself and His ways. And know that your **obedience** is not just for *your* sake. Let's be used by the Lord and see what He does through us!

The Eighth Day – New Beginnings

As we reach Leviticus 9, we have made it to the **eighth day** of the ceremony. Remember, offering the burnt offering, putting the blood on the right ear, right thumb, right big toe, offering the wave offering telling the Lord that they were *completely* dependent on Him, and the anointment with oil (signifying the Holy Spirit was on them) happened *daily* for seven days as part of the ordination service. This is the setting as we get to Leviticus 9. They have just completed that seven-day course of ordination.

Read Leviticus 9:1-2. "On the **eighth** day." Before we go any farther, what is significant about *eight* in the Bible? The Jews say it is the number for **new beginnings**. Why? The dedication of the firstborn to God happens on the **eighth** day (Exodus 22:29-30). Circumcision happens on the **eighth** day (Leviticus 12:3). Purification of skin disease (leprosy) happens on the **eighth** day (Leviticus 14:10). Purification of a bodily discharge happens on the **eighth** day (Leviticus 15:14, 29). You may sacrifice animals once they are **eight** days old (Leviticus 22:27). The purification of a defiled Nazirite occurs on the **eighth** day (Numbers 6:10, 29:35).

On the eight day, Aaron and his sons were to offer a **sin offering** and a **burnt offering**. For this sin offering, he was to offer a **calf** and a **bull**. Tell me God doesn't have a sense of humor. The *first* animal Aaron was to sacrifice was a calf. I just picture Aaron when he gave that offering. I see him imagining the man-made golden calf that he had the people worship in the not-so-distant past. And now God was allowing Him to be the high priest as he offered a calf for an offering. In addition to this sin offering, he was to offer a **burnt offering** of a **ram**. These two offerings were specifically for *Aaron and his sons*.

Next, there needed to be offerings made on behalf of the people. Verses 3-4 tell us the offerings that were to be made for Israel. What were they? **Sin offering, burnt offering, peace offering, and grain offering**. That is almost every offering we have discussed so far! There is only one offering previously discussed that did not need to be given. The **guilt offering**. The reason that a guilt offering wasn't given is that it is a *private* offering made specifically by the worshipper. It is not an appropriate offering to give on behalf of all of Israel.

What was the *reason* behind all of these offerings? Look at verse 4. The text says, "**Today** the **Lord** will appear to you." These are the only words emphasized in the entire chapter in the original Hebrew language! As a matter of fact, this is repeated in verse 6. You see, these offerings were not some mindless traditions that God wanted His people doing. The people were not at the Tabernacle just going through motions. **Today**, God was going to show up if they just obeyed!

Continuing through the chapter, verses 7 through 21 specifically talk about how Aaron obeyed what the Lord had spoken through Moses *precisely*. Do you think he wanted God to show up? Absolutely!

Jump down to **verse 22**. Do you *see* Aaron lifting his hands? When you read God's Word, get there on the scene! The text says that he *blessed* the people after making the offerings. What does that mean? *Blessed* here (*barak*) means *to pass on benefit.* Look at **Deuteronomy 10:8**. God wanted His representatives (priests) to *bless in His name.* Know that **blessings** have been spoken when God's people get together since the time of Moses. What did these blessings look like? Turn to **Numbers 6:23-27**. To this very day, the only people that know their Jewish lineage are those who descended from the line of Aaron. They are called *Kohenim.* These are direct descendants of the priestly class. Multiple times a year in synagogues, a *Kohen* will pronounce the blessing of Numbers 6 over the people. Jesus Himself pronounced a *blessing* over the disciples in **Luke 24:50-53**. He was likely reciting the words of Numbers 6 to them as He was taken up to Heaven.

Now, *who* was doing the blessing in Leviticus 9? Was it Aaron or was it God? Aaron is the conduit, but God is the One doing the blessing. Aaron was God's representative. Again, get on the scene here. If you live in this culture, what is the greatest blessing that a person could have? Is it more money? Is it a bigger house? Is it more stuff? No! We tend to think "blessing" is *material* things. That is not even on these peoples' radar screens. A blessing in this culture revolved around one thing – the **addition of descendants**. If you look at every text that talks about *blessing* in the Old Testament, the most frequent thing it is talking about is *descendants* or *fertility*...and there isn't a close second!

Read verse 23. Aaron and Moses went into the Tent of Meeting together. This is the first time anyone has gone into the Tent of Meeting since Exodus 40 when the glory of the Lord *filled* the Tabernacle so much that Moses could not even enter. Until this point, Moses was the only one who could approach God. If you are an Israelite there that day witnessing all of this, I am sure you had goosebumps. This is huge. And then they come back out. Our text says that they **blessed** the people again, and the **glory of the Lord appeared**. *Glory (kābôd)* means *weight* or *heaviness.* This same phrase is used in Exodus 24 when it talks about the **glory of the Lord appearing at Mount Sinai**. This same phrase is also used in Exodus 40 when the **glory of the Lord filled the Tabernacle**. Do you understand that this was no accident by God? He wanted His people to understand that the Tabernacle was a *portable Sinai.* As His glory shows up yet again at the inauguration of the priesthood, He is essentially putting His stamp of approval on the sacrificial system we have been talking about since we started Leviticus a couple of months ago.

So God showed up. It was the fulfillment of verses 4 and 6. "**Today** the **Lord** will appear to you"! He did!

Read verse 24. Over and over in the Bible, one of the pictures of God is **fire**. We have talked about this before in our covenant lesson. Just a few examples in the Old Testament for those interested – Ex. 3:2, Ex. 19:18, Dt. 4:24, Ps. 18:8-14, Isa. 33:14, Ezek. 1:4, and Mal. 3:2. When God is present and at work, there is often **fire**. Think about the New Testament. John the Baptist promised that Jesus could come and baptize with the Holy Spirit and **fire** (Matt. 3:11). The Day of Pentecost in Acts 2:3, we see the Holy Spirit make Himself known as **tongues of fire**. Jesus even says that He came to send **fire** on the earth and that He wished it were already kindled (Luke 12:49). **Fire** accompanies the presence of God. He *is* a consuming fire (Hebrews 12:29).

Knowing that God showed up among them, how did the people respond? First, they **shouted**. It is the Hebrew word *rānan*. It is a *joyful shout of elation*. Almost every other time this word is used in Scripture, it is translated as **joy**. And *this* is the first time this used in Scripture. Always pay attention to the first place that a word is used in Scripture! It will teach you God's definition of that word. In this case, **joy** is what is expressed when a person comes in direct contact with Him. It is no different for us. Do you know where true joy is found today? It is in the person of Jesus Christ. It is a *fruit of the Spirit*. You see, when we are constantly in contact with Jesus and allow the Holy Spirit to work in our lives, **joy** is what is expressed! It's a joy that can't be hidden. It's a joy that is not dependent on circumstance. And it is a joy that can't be contained! Do others see that type of joy flowing out of your life? If not, I would ask this hard question. *How connected are you to the person of Jesus Christ? Are you abiding in Him? Are you allowing the Holy Spirit to flow through you?* It is only in these times that **joy** will be truly expressed.

There is something else the people did besides *shout for joy*. The text says that they **fell on their faces**. We see this time and again. When God makes His presence known, there is *one* response. To fall on our face as we understand who *we* are and who *He* is. It is a posture of respect and awe. We fall on our faces when we are *overwhelmed* with the fact that we are in someone else's company. Have you ever really thought about that moment you meet Jesus and you see His face for the very first time? I have thought about it. I love songs like "I Can Only Imagine." *Will I stand in your presence or to my knees will I fall?* If you look at **Revelation 4:10-11**, you get an idea of what we will be doing when we see Him. The twenty-four elders will **fall down** before Him who sits on the throne, and will **worship Him** who lives forever and ever, and will **cast their crowns** before the throne... I love this text. The twenty-four elders threw their *crowns* at His feet. Even their accolades belonged to the Lord. And they worshipped Him and told Him how amazing He is. *I hope you look forward to the moment you meet Jesus as much as I do!*

You know, there is a reason Jews pray as they do. Do you know *how* Jews pray? Their posture is called "shucklen." They rock back and forth. It is interesting to know where this posture came from. There are two reasons they do it. We won't get into great detail about the second reason, but the main reason is that, originally, Jews would completely go face down every time the name of God was mentioned. But His name is all over the place. So, instead, they began just rocking back and forth in a motion of respect. A slight bow as they recite His word or pray to Him. Why? If you are in His presence, their thought is that you should show respect. The second reason they do this is because of Proverbs 20:27 which says,

"The soul of man is a ***candle*** *of God."* So, they want to mimic a flame that constantly sways back and forth since they are a candle to God.

These two expressions balance each other out, right? Being *joyful* and being *overwhelmed* at the same time. **Psalm 2:11** says, "*Worship the Lord with reverence, and rejoice with trembling.*" There is a balance in our walk with Christ. We are to **joyfully worship Him** as He shows us His will. We are to respond appropriately by doing *exactly* what He tells us to do. However, we will never be obedient to joyfully worship Him if we do not have the **reverence** and **trembling** of who He is. Do you remember Ananias and Sapphira in Acts 5? What did they do wrong? They sold land and pretended that they gave the apostles *all* of the money. Why did they sell the land? At the end of Acts 4, Barnabas does the same thing. Barnabas is a man *sold out* for Christ. Ananias and Sapphira are more interested in *looking holy* and *being holy*. What did God do to them? He struck them down. Do you know the response of the people? It says that there was **great fear**. See, Ananias and Sapphira wanted to look the part without being the real deal. Listen, do you get it? We should **fear** trying to *play church*. We should **fear** trying to deceive God. We should **fear** acting like church is a game to be played. We should **fear** trivializing Christ's sacrifice.

Fear is an element that is necessary if we are going to **joyfully worship Him** in complete obedience.

All of this happened on the **eighth day** of the priestly ordination. It was a day of **new beginnings** as there was a new High Priest that would be a representative of God to the people and a representative of the people to God. Maybe you need a new beginning. Maybe you are living a life that trivializes the sacrifice of Christ. Maybe you have made church into a game to be played. There is good news. Jesus loves to give new beginnings. He loves hearts that realize their error and He loves when His people turn to Him.

Doing Things My Way

In chapter 9, we talked about the **eighth day** of the priestly ordination service. As we reach Leviticus 10, it is still the **eighth day**. It is still the same day that God showed up among the people.

Last week, the Intermediate School had awards day. One of the awards that both of my oldest children, Brylee and Nolan, received was the *math* award for their class. I can already see that my third child, Neely, really likes math as well. They all get it honestly. Julie and I both really liked math when we were in school. Now, I took a *lot* of math classes in school. Of all of those classes, I think the best preparation in using simple math didn't come from learning it in a classroom. The best preparation came, of all places, on a golf course. See, when you play high school golf, much of your time consists of figuring up scores. On a given hole, you have to not only keep up with *your* score, but you better keep up with the score of your three playing partners as well. Why? *Because many of the other players often have a hard time adding up **all** of their strokes!*

The rules of golf are very clear...you must add up **every time** you hit the golf ball. So why do you think there is so much confusion on the next tee box as each score gets recorded on the scorecard? *It's simple. People want to play by their **own** rules to make themselves look better.* Let's dive into Leviticus 10.

> ***Now Nadab and Abihu, the sons of Aaron, took their respective firepans, and after putting fire in them, placed incense on it and offered strange fire before the LORD, which He had not commanded them. And fire came out from the presence of the LORD and consumed them, and they died before the LORD.***
> **Leviticus 10:1-2**

Setting: Can you imagine the spiritual "mountain top" these people were on during the **eighth day**? The God of the Universe was among them! And amid this joyful, incredible moment, tragedy struck! It was the **first** fire offering by the new priests (Nadab and Abihu) when they were struck down because they offered **strange fire** to the Lord. So many times in Scripture, we see examples of temptations and falls on the heels of mountain top experiences. Even Jesus was tempted by the enemy just after being baptized. The same thing often happens today. We may be tempted shortly after having a spiritual high. Why do you think this happens so often? We have an enemy that wants to bring us down! He knows that when we are passionately pursuing what Christ has for us, the Lord will work through us. If he can just take our eyes off of Jesus (even momentarily), it will have an impact. He often goes after us the hardest when we are growing spiritually. If you are growing in your walk with Christ right now, I want to give you a word of caution – *watch out for the enemy! He wants to take your eyes off of Jesus. He wants to slow your roll when it comes to your impact for Christ. Keep focused on Jesus!*

Characters: Who were Nadab and Abihu? They were Aaron's oldest sons (Exodus 6:23). Think about all they had seen in their life. They saw first-hand the miracles that God had performed to bring their people out of Egypt. They witnessed what happened when the glory of the Lord showed up on Mount Sinai. The smoke. The fire. The lightening. They had felt the earthquake and the thunder along with all the other Israelites (Exodus 19). They were *there* at Mount Sinai worshipping the Lord from a distance with Moses and the seventy elders (Exodus 24). Wouldn't you think that experience would have given them a healthy *fear* of the Lord? We talked about the importance of having this type of fear in chapter 9 as we discussed Ananias and Sapphira. Their story is so very similar to Nadab and Abihu. Just because we have a "mountain top" experience with the Lord doesn't mean we can't make sinful decisions in the valley! *Keep your eyes on Jesus at all times. Listen to His voice. Obey Him!*

Offered: There is something very important to understand about the offering they gave the Lord. The text says they **offered** strange fire. The Hebrew word for *offered* used here is *qareb*. We have talked about this word before. It means *to draw near **expecting** a significant result.* As these men drew near to God to give these offerings to the Him (that He never prescribed), they **expected** God to *accept* them and *bless* them. *They never imagined the result they would receive!* Last night, we stopped at Dairy Queen. Julie ordered a cookie dough blizzard. That is **not** what she received. Do you think she was happy about getting something different than what she said she wanted? *These two men whipped God up a different blizzard than He asked for and **expected** Him to be excited about the new flavor. But that is not what He asked for!*

Strange fire: Let's talk about this **strange fire** that the priests, Nadab and Abihu, offered to the Lord. God had given *very specific instructions* for the offerings He expected from the priests. He left nothing to the imagination. But these two men decided to give Him an offering to *their* specifications rather than *His*. This strange fire has been debated for centuries. Jewish scholars have proposed twelve theories of what this strange fire might have been. We are not going to get into all of these theories, but we know that they did not offer precisely what God had asked them to offer. It was **strange**. The NIV and ESV translates it as **unauthorized**. The New Living Translation really makes it clear when it says: "*they disobeyed the LORD by burning before him the **wrong kind of fire**, different than he had commanded*." *How often do I give God **strange** offerings? How often do I give Him offerings that are **different** than what He commanded me to give? Much like those high school golfers that we talked about at the beginning of the lesson, how often do I make up my own rules to make myself look good? How often do I work hard "in His name" completing tasks that He never asked me to complete? How often do I expect Him to pat me on the back for my service to Him when He never called me to that specific service?*

God's Response: In response to these men giving an offering He never asked for, He killed them. Why? *When God gives His people specific instructions, He **expects** us to follow them precisely!* The text does not say that they gave Him a *bad* offering. It does not say that they gave Him a *half-hearted* offering. It says that they gave Him a **strange** offering...an offering that did not match His instructions. Now, **how** did He kill them? *"**Fire** came out from the presence of the Lord and consumed them."* Please don't miss this. This is the **same** fire that we see in Leviticus 9:24 (just two verses earlier). What was the fire doing then? We talked about this in Leviticus 8. That fire was God's stamp of approval on the sacrificial system. It was a fire of celebration! And now? The same fire came in **judgment**. **Fire** often accompanies the presence of God. If you add up all the verses in Scripture where fire shows up representing God, exactly half of them show the fire in a beneficial way (like in Leviticus 9:24) and the other half show the fire as a form of **judgment**. A few other examples for those interested: Ex. 24:17, Dt. 5:22, Num 11:1, Num 16:35, 2 Kings 1:10, 12. See, Deuteronomy 4:24 says, *"For the Lord your God is a **consuming fire**, a **jealous God**."* We read things about God being **jealous**, and think, *"God, didn't you say that we are **not** supposed to be jealous?"* Then, we turn to James 3:16 and read, *"For where **jealousy** and selfish ambition exist, there is disorder and every evil thing.**"*** So, we think thoughts like, "God, did you forget what you wrote in Your Word?" Um, no. He did not. See, God has a **right** to jealousy. Think about it this way. If you are God. Is it *loving* to allow people to worship things other than you? No! God created each of us. He *longs* for us to choose Him rather than the enemy. He *longs* to be the One we worship. You better believe that He is **jealous** for us and for our worship. But that is a very different type of jealousy than what we often exhibit, isn't it? We are jealous for material things, mainly. God is a **jealous** God and He is a **consuming fire**.

Read 1 Corinthians 3:10-15. There is a day coming in which this same fire that either **approved** of the Israelite's actions in Leviticus 9 or **judged** their actions in Leviticus 10 will one day be put to *our works*. The text says that the fire will judge the **quality** of each man's work. Everything you do either is from the Lord or it isn't. There is no in between. As we reach Heaven, God's fire will reveal the source of your actions. Were they from *you* or were they from the *Lord*? His fire will either *consume* your works (if they weren't from Him) or the works will remain despite the fire (if they were from Him).

In Leviticus 10, don't miss the heart of what these priests did. They acted in complete disregard for God. He gave them specific instructions of what *He* wanted, and they gave him the offering that seemed more pleasing to *them*. They didn't want to play by *His* rules, they wanted Him to play by *their* rules. How many times do I do the same thing? How many times do I do what I want to do and then ask God to bless it rather than allowing Him to be Lord and doing what He has told me to do? Guess what...if we do what He tells us to do, He *will* bless it because He is the One that instructed it. There are no bonus points in doing things "in His Name" when He isn't the One who told us to do those things! And there is a day coming when **all** will know if your actions are truly from the Lord. You can't fake it when the heat of God's fire examines the quality of your works. You can fake it now. You can make people think you are a "good Christian." But there is a day coming when the truth will be revealed.

Do you understand how important it is to get this right? God killed two men for their strange offerings that He never asked for! Do not dare come to Him with a careless attitude! Instead, our ears must listen closely to His voice and obey Him precisely! We cannot do things our way...we must do them His way!

As we finish, I want you to look at the very next verse with me. **Read Leviticus 10:3**. God says that He *will* be treated as **holy**. This word is written in the *imperfect tense* which means it is never ending. God will be treated as holy by everyone, including *us*! If you are a believer in Jesus Christ, God says that He will not stand for you to treat Him as something *common*. If you approach Him as though He isn't holy, there will be consequences. The text continues by saying that before all the people, He *will* be **honored**. We talked about this word last week. It is the word for *weight* or *heaviness*. It is also in the *imperfect tense.* God will be honored by everyone, forever. Including us!

Are you treating God as **holy**? It is easy to say, "Well, yes. I go to church every Sunday. I pray. I read the Bible." But God says that *if* you are to treat Him as **holy**, *you* will be holy yourself. Look at **Leviticus 11:44**. God's people were to be **holy** since He was **holy**. It says the same thing in 1 Peter 1:14-16: *As obedient children, do not be conformed to the former lusts which were yours in your ignorance, but like the Holy One who called you, be holy yourselves also in all your behavior; because it is written, "YOU SHALL BE HOLY, FOR I AM HOLY."* If we are not set apart and different, we cannot say that we are treating God as **holy**.

God also says that He will be **honored**. Are you **honoring** God? Again, we talked about this word in Leviticus 9. Do you remember when it said that the **glory** of the Lord appeared to them? That was the Hebrew word *kābôḏ.* Three verses later, God says that all the people will *kābēḏ* Him. It is the exact same root. See, the way we **honor** Him is the same way the people **honored** Him at the end of Leviticus 9 when the *kābôḏ* of the Lord showed up. What did they do? They *worshipped* (shouted with joy) and *feared Him* (fell on their faces). They lived out **Psalm 2:11**. This is how we live a life that *honors* Him.

Will you continuously treat Him as **holy**? If so, your life should be set apart. Not just to look different, but to be set apart to do the works that He calls you to. Will you continuously treat Him as **honored**? Will you live a life that is full of *joy* and a healthy *fear* of Him because you understand who He is and who you are?

Kosher Lives

**The Lord spoke again to Moses and to Aaron, saying to them, "Speak to the sons of Israel, saying, `These are the creatures which you may eat from all the animals that are on the earth.' "
Leviticus 11:1-2**

We are going to examine *kosher laws*. The Hebrew word for it is *kashrut*. Leviticus 11 gives to most details about kosher laws in the Bible. While we are not going to break all of them down in great detail, we need to understand kosher laws because there are some principles that apply to us as Christians today.

In Leviticus 11, God says that some animals, birds, fish, and insects were considered acceptable to eat while others were not. There are four basic divisions in this chapter. Land animals (vv. 1-8), Water animals (vv. 9-12), flying animals (vv. 13-23), and swarming animals (vv. 29-31). The other place in the Bible that contains some dietary laws is Deuteronomy 14.

Now, **why** did He set these limits of *kosher laws*? There are many theories. Philo theorized that animals represented something spiritual and God was using it as an allegory. Others thought God was wanting to limit how many animals were killed. Many have subscribed to the theory of hygiene, meaning that God was protecting His people from certain diseases. But it becomes tough to take this stand completely when you think about some of the verses we will discuss later from the New Testament. The real reason for *kosher laws* was almost assuredly because *unclean animals* were those that were known to have played a role in pagan religion. If God's people had nothing to do with those animals, it would be a statement that Israel was **different** than the other religions. She was set apart. In Israel, you didn't have to guess who an *Israelite* was and who was a *pagan*. Their diet would tell the world that they were **different** but also that they were **supremely committed to their covenant with God**.

As we think about these kosher laws, I want you to turn to something that Jesus says in **Mark 7:14-15**. The setting for this text is that some Jesus disciples were eating bread with "impure hands." They had not practiced *netilat yadayim* according to their traditions. This is still practiced today by Jews. They pour water two to three times on each hand and recite a blessing – "*Blessed are You, Lord our God, King of the universe, who has sanctified us with Your commandments, and commanded us concerning the washing of hands.*" This was not a tradition about hygiene. You had to do this even if you had clean hands. After reciting the blessing, you do not speak until you pick up the bread and recite the blessing for it. Listen, Jesus was a Torah-observant Jew. He says that He did not come to *abolish* the Law, but to fulfill it (Matt. 5:17). We hear that and think, "Jesus is saying that He has already fulfilled the requirements of the Law so we don't have to worry about those things anymore." No! That would have meant that He *abolished* the Law. See, the root of this text is saying that Jesus came to "make full" (*plerosai*) the Law. He came to interpret God's Laws correctly and show us how to live them out!

As Christians, we often look at another passage incorrectly based on extremely poor translations. Look at **Romans 10:4**. The NASB says that Jesus is the *end* of the Law of righteousness to everyone who believes. The problem is that the Greek word for "end" is *telos*. It used **42** times in Scripture. The work means *result* or *outcome* or *completion*. When we read Romans 10:4 as Christians and *think* that it is saying that, if you believe in Jesus, you no longer have to worry about the Law. Just throw away the Old Testament and its 627 laws that God made way back then. Just focus on the New Testament. However, listen to how the verse should read: *For the **goal** at which the Torah aims is the Messiah, who offers righteousness to everyone who believes.*

Jesus came, not to **abolish** what we see about kosher laws in Leviticus 11. He came to teach us what the heart of God's Law on kosher laws was supposed to tell us about Him. He came to show us how to live out God's Word correctly.

In Mark 7, Jesus was raising the idea of **kosher** to a new level. The Pharisees were saying that the disciples should have washed their hands before eating the bread. They should have practiced the man-made pharisee tradition of *netilat yadayim*. The food, itself, was *kosher*. However, according to the Pharisee's traditions of the time, if a person took food without practicing *netilat yadayim*, that food became *unclean* (*nonkosher*). Jesus is telling them that their *traditions* (that were not from God) were ridiculous. In Mark 7, Jesus does go on to declare all foods *clean*, but He "ups the ante" of *kosher laws* by saying it's what comes **out** of a person's heart that makes them *unclean*. It's not just some dietary practice. Spiritual *cleanness* involves your heart, not just your stomach.

There is another text involving the idea of kosher laws that I want us to look at today. Turn to **Acts 10:9-16**. Peter has this vision of a large sheet coming down from Heaven filled with unclean food. You *must* get the context of this verse. We look at these verses and think the only thing it is talking about is us eating food that had previously been considered unclean. No! This verse is in the middle of the story about a Gentile centurion named Cornelius. Peter is a Jew. Can a Gentile come to a Jew's home? Absolutely not. Initially, God wanted His people completely *separate* because He didn't want them to worship foreign gods when they made it to the promised land. So, He told them to be different. Don't eat what they eat. Don't associate with them because you may become like them. Then, we get to the New Testament. Cornelius may be a Gentile, but he is a **god-fearing** Gentile. God needed to do something to wake Peter up to the fact that what used to be *unclean* is now *clean*. What did He use? Food! See, Peter knew about the dietary laws. He knew some things were absolutely *unclean* and he had to stay away from those things. In the vision, God showed Peter that what used to be *unclean* is now *clean*. His primary focus was not really food! That vision was telling Peter that the Gentiles (who used to be unclean) were now clean. After talking with Cornelius, Peter gets it. How do we know? Look at **verses 34 and 35**. Gentiles were now *kosher* for salvation.

We said earlier that there were different theories as to *why* God created kosher laws. One thought was that it was for the purpose of hygiene. Jesus, Himself, says that He has made all food *clean*. If it was simply about hygiene and health, why would Jesus tell us today that it is fine to eat whatever we want? Does He not love us as much as He did the Israelites of the Old Testament? Instead, these dietary laws are a matter of *holiness* and *separation*. They were created to make Israel *different* and *set apart* from those they came in contact with.

Let's take a look at **Leviticus 11:44-45**.

> *For I am the LORD your God. Consecrate yourselves therefore, and be holy, for I am holy. And you shall not make yourselves unclean with any of the swarming things that swarm on the earth.*
> **Leviticus 11:44**

Let me tell you a little story of a time when I was in college at the University of Tennessee working for the football team. It was a hot, grueling practice. Not just for the football players, but for the equipment staff, too! As we came into the equipment room, I spoke up about a fellow manager *not* giving his best effort at practice. Then, the piercing statement from another manager was uttered which I can still hear very clearly to this day:

> *"Well, isn't that the pot calling the kettle black?"*

While the statement stung, I knew that it was true. **That day, in the equipment room at UT, God taught me a lesson about the importance of being set apart.**

We have been talking about dietary laws that spell out *unclean* things for the Israelites. Yes, there were specific things that God ordered them to stay away from! But I want to turn our focus on a couple of instructions God spelled out towards the end of the chapter.

<u>Consecrate</u> yourselves therefore, and be holy, for I am holy.

God told His people to *consecrate (qāash)* themselves. This word means to *be set apart, sharing the likeness of nature with God*. The Lord is not only telling His people to **separate *from* sin**, but He is also telling them to **separate *to* Himself**. This is such an important distinction. I can stay *away from* sin, but am I *running to* God? This reminds me of a lesson I learned just outside of Bethlehem in Israel. Ray Vander Laan had us spend about 20 minutes cleaning rocks out of a field. Then, he gathered all of us up. He asked us, "What are the rocks that need to be removed from the field of your heart so that you can grow spiritually?" Then, he told us a story. It was in this same field that he had been to years before. In this same field, God had told him that he was watching too much NFL football. He told the Lord on that day that he would remove the rock of football because he was wasting so much time watching it. He came back home after the trip. The first weekend of NFL football arrived, and he didn't watch a minute of it. Do you know what he did instead? He slept. It was then that he realized that it didn't do any good to give up football if he didn't fill that time with something for the Lord. So, he told his wife that they would come up with a plan for Sundays that involved spending time with the Lord in place of watching football. See, we are not only be separated **from** something, but we are to be separated **to** someone. This is consecration.

And you shall not make yourselves <u>unclean</u> with any of the swarming things that swarm on the earth.

God warned His people to *not* make themselves *unclean (āmē')*. This word means to be *unclean from spiritual contamination*. The Lord had specifically said for the Israelites to stay away from "swarming things that swarm on the earth." Therefore, if they did not obey, they became **unclean**. Understand that this word is written in the *piel stem* which focuses on the **impact of the action**. Now, what was the impact of an Israelite who was *unclean*? **They were unfit for His service!**

*For us to be used for the Lord's kingdom, we must be **consecrated**. This is so much more than separating from sin; it means we must be running **towards** God! Not only that, there are things in life that we must keep our distance from. Why? The impact of those things will **destroy our witness**, rendering that which we are proclaiming void.*

That hot day at football practice, my work ethic was pathetic. You see, I wasn't working with *all* my heart as though I was doing it for the Lord (Colossians 3:23). As a matter of fact, my work was just as lazy as all the other managers. I wasn't *set apart* at all. That day, the Lord showed me the importance of living a life that is *set apart* for His glory! He showed me what it means to live a *kosher* life.

Over and over in the New Testament, Paul alludes to the kosher laws. Instead of using them to talk about food, he uses the language to talk about believers *sinning*. We see it in Romans 6:9, 2 Corinthians 12:21, Ephesians 4:19, Ephesians 5:3, 5, 1 Thessalonians 4:7. The clearest time he refers to it is in 2 Corinthians 6:17 when he quotes Leviticus 11.

It is time we start living lives that are *kosher*. It is time we start living lives in which the *unclean* is removed and the sin is cut out. It is time we start not just viewing our salvation as a life separate **from** sin. Instead, we view our salvation as a life separate **to** God. Do you really want to impact this world for the Kingdom of God? Take this lesson seriously. Be holy as He is holy. Identify the unclean areas that need to be removed. And follow Him with all of your heart, all of your soul, all of your strength, and all of your mind.

The Reason Simeon and Anna Met Jesus

I like to tell people that I have given birth to four children. My wife thinks I am crazy, but the Bible teaches that we are one. So, the way I figure it, *we* have given birth to four children. That includes *me*. Hence, I have given birth to four children. Leviticus 12 teaches about the laws for purification for a new mom. We are going to essentially cover the entire chapter together.

Let's go ahead and read **Leviticus 12**. Over and over in Scripture, we see the idea of *pain* in childbirth mentioned. We even see the *process* of childbirth discussed in multiple areas of the Bible. However, *this* is the only place where purification of birth is mentioned.

There are three sections:

1. **Purification** after birth of a **son** (vv. 1-4).
2. **Purification** after birth of a **daughter** (v. 5).
3. **Sacrificial offerings** after childbirth (vv. 6-8).

Before we dive into these sections, let me ask you a question. *Why* did there need to be purification after childbirth? From everything we have discussed in Leviticus, and everything you know about the Law, why did God require purification? I mean, God gave us the mandate to be fruitful, multiply, and fill the Earth. Right? So why does He require *purification* when fulfilling this mandate? The reason is that the mom comes in contact with **blood** while she is giving birth. Therefore, she is defiled. The text even says that she is unclean "as in the days of her menstruation" (v. 2).

Birth of Son:

A mom is unclean for seven days after giving birth to a son. What all is involved with **spiritual uncleanness**? If you look at **Leviticus 15:19-24**, you will see what she can't do. It is the same as when she is menstruating. If anyone touches her, they are unclean. Whatever she lies on, it becomes unclean. Whatever she sits on becomes unclean. If someone even touches the bed or chair that she has been on, they become unclean. On the eighth day, what happens to the boy? He is circumcised. This is not the first time God has said to circumcise a boy on the eighth day. Do you know where to find the first time He gives this command? **Genesis 17:12**. After the boy is circumcised, she had to wait an additional *thirty-three* days to be purified from her bleeding (v. 4). During those *thirty-three* days, she could not touch any holy object or even enter the tabernacle for a total of **forty days**. She was spiritually separated and could not worship God with others! This is a big deal. In Leviticus 11, we discussed kosher laws. We discussed that the New Testament uses the same language of kosher laws when talking about believers and sin. If we are dabbling in sin, we become *spiritually unclean*. Yes, I am thankful for God's grace when I mess up. But just because He is merciful doesn't give me the liberty to take advantage of His character. This new mom can't worship God for almost **6 weeks** after giving birth. In their culture, spiritual uncleanness and spiritual separation were two of the worst things a person could experience. Then, we get to the New Testament where Jesus, Peter, and Paul all equate *sin* with making the believer *spiritually unclean*. Do you understand how important it is for us to **flee** from sin? I never realized how many places in Scripture talk about fleeing sin! Ecclesiastes 21, Amos 5, 1 Corinthians 6, 1 Corinthians 10, 1 Timothy 6. and 2 Timothy 2 all tell us to flee from certain types of sin. Our fellowship with the Lord is at stake. I don't know about you, but I want to be **spiritually clean**. I want to be able to approach the Lord with a pure heart that is free from dirt. Know that, after childbirth, new moms did not have that right for almost 6 weeks.

Birth of Daughter:

How long was a mom spiritually unclean after giving birth to a daughter? She was unclean for the first two weeks, then she was spiritually separated for an additional sixty-six days. It is a total of **80** days. You don't have to be a genius to figure out that God made mom spiritually unclean **twice** the amount of time if she had a daughter rather than a son. *Why* would this be the case? You can look at Jewish records over the years and see there have been many thoughts. Some thought it was because girls are sometimes smaller than boys and would need more time of personal care with their mom to survive. Others taught that a mom would have discharge after birth longer if she had a girl than a boy, so that accounted for the extra time. Still, others said it was because God cursed *women* with painful childbirth due to the fall. God made the punishment of a longer period of uncleanness when a *girl* was born. Let me make one thing very clear. Some people say the Bible points to more *value* being placed on men than women. Some even point to different laws such as the purity law to make their point. In no way was this a statement that one sex was greater than the other. How do we know? As we will see in just a few minutes, the sacrifices that the mother was to offer were the **same** whether she had a boy or a girl. Genders were considered *equal* (yet different) to God.

It is obvious why God only gave moms of boys *seven* days of uncleanness. On the eighth day, he was circumcised. If mom was unclean, she couldn't attend the ceremony because she couldn't be around other people. But nobody knows why the time is *doubled* with the birth of a girl. Last week, we talked about the idea of *kosher laws* helped Israel stay set apart from the Canaanites. God didn't want His people even messing with animals involved in the worship of their gods. I can't help but think that the laws on purity after childbirth may have the same reasoning behind it. You see, Canaanite gods and pagan gods at this time almost always revolved around the idea of *reproduction*. The people thought that the gods lived in the underworld. The Greek name for that is *Hades*. The Hebrew name for it is *Sheol*. They believed these gods came out in the spring to procreate if the people were doing the right religious practices. I went to Caesarea Philippi two years ago and stood on rocks in the very place where these pagans performed these practices. See, they believed that the gods came out in the spring, had sex with each other, and the spring rain was the sperm that caused growth on the ground. But what was their role? How did they get these gods to come out? They would have elaborate ceremonies at the base of where they believed these gods came out that involved huge orgies. Men with women. Women with women. Men with men. And people with animals. This was the culture. God says, "I want to create a system in which people understand that *I* am the giver of life and not some nasty religious practice." He wanted women to stay home and *away* from tabernacle for a period of time after giving birth. And that period of time was even *longer* if she had a female as if to say, "One day these girls will have children of their own. *I* am the One who produces fertility in these girls, not religious practices."

Sacrificial Offerings after Childbirth:

When the days of her purification are completed, for a son or for a daughter, she shall bring to the priest at the doorway of the tent of meeting a one year old lamb for a burnt offering and a young pigeon or a turtledove for a sin offering. Then he shall offer it before the LORD and make atonement for her, and she shall be cleansed from the flow of her blood. This is the law for her who bears a child, whether a male or a female.
Leviticus 12:6-7

After the period of separation, the new mom had to offer a sacrifice. She was to bring a year-old lamb for a burnt offering and a pigeon or dove for a sin offering. Once these offerings were made, she became *clean*.

Why have this offering? I mean, we know she didn't sin by having a child (like we talked about earlier). It is an issue of the blood. Leviticus 17:11 – *"For the life of the flesh is in the blood."* The loss of blood required purification. The mom lost *life* during the process of childbirth and the period of time afterward when she was losing blood. Requiring an offering for this event allows God to remind His people of the importance of the life-giving aspect of blood.

I *love* the account of Simeon and Anna meeting Jesus in the temple just after His birth. Simeon had been told by the Holy Spirit that he would not die before seeing the Messiah (Luke 2:26). What an amazing moment it must have been as he laid eyes on Jesus! At 84 years old, Anna spent day and night in the temple. When she saw Jesus, she began to *bear witness* to what she had seen (Luke 2:38)! But, did you know that Simeon and Anna would have never met the Messiah without Leviticus 12?

Listen to *why* Mary and Joseph had to go to the temple that day.

*"And when the **days for their purification according to the law of Moses** were completed, they brought Him up to Jerusalem to present Him to the Lord (**as it is written in the Law of the Lord**, 'EVERY firstborn MALE THAT OPENS THE WOMB SHALL BE*

> *CALLED HOLY TO THE LORD'), and to offer a **sacrifice** according*
> *to what was said in the Law of the Lord, 'A **PAIR OF***
> ***TURTLEDOVES OR TWO YOUNG PIGEONS**.' " Luke 2:22-24*

Don't miss a key element of this passage. It says that Mary and Joseph offered a *"pair of turtledoves or two young pigeons."* I thought the text said they were to offer a year-old lamb and a pigeon or dove. Well, there was *one* exception. **Read verse 8**.

Our Christian artwork typically depicts Mary and Joseph heading to Bethlehem on a donkey. Only the *rich* owned donkeys. Mary and Joseph were not rich. As a matter of fact, they were poor. The Christmas story begins with a 90-mile hike from Nazareth to Bethlehem through the desert. That doesn't change the message, but we need to understand the context. It matters. They get to Bethlehem. There was no room in the inn. Jesus is born in a manger. Do you get this picture? Jesus left Heaven to come to a nasty, smelly, gross world. He was born in a water trough in a shepherd's cave. And He was born to parents that were in the poorest class of people in their world. This is what **humbling yourself** looks like!

After Jesus' birth, Mary is *unclean* for the first seven days. Then comes day **8**. A **burnt offering** and a **sin offering** were required for a Mary to make atonement because of Leviticus 12. They head to Jerusalem for these offerings. By the way - the word *atonement* (in Leviticus 12:7) literally means *a shielding substitute*. Imagine the scene in Luke 2. The mother of Jesus is giving a blood offering of a couple of birds to be a *shielding substitute* for the birth of Jesus. How is that for irony?

*My wife and I did not have to go up to the church and sacrifice a couple of birds for atonement after each of our kids was born. Thankfully, the baby that Mary offered the sacrifice for that day at the temple grew up, died on a cross, and became **my** sacrifice. He provides constant **atonement** for those of us who trust Him.*

All of this to say that God's perfect plan never fails. Because of a sacrifice God commanded His people to perform years before, Simeon and Anna met the Messiah.

Every second of *my* life has been ordered by God. God *knew* Simeon and Anna would meet Jesus that day when He gave the commandment for purification after childbirth. In the very same way, He has a perfect plan for my life (and for your life) and He is not making it up as He goes.

Will we trust Him with our every step?

A Clean Bill of Health

Then the LORD spoke to Moses and to Aaron, saying, "When a man has on the skin of his body a swelling or a scab or a bright spot, and it becomes an infection of leprosy on the skin of his body, then he shall be brought to Aaron the priest or to one of his sons the priests."
Leviticus 13:1-2

Leviticus 13 has a topic that is not always translated into English the same way. Some translations say *leprosy* and others say something like a *serious skin disease.* The Hebrew word used here is *tzara'at.* It is a general word for a skin condition that could many anything from psoriasis to a fungal infection. We see different instructions based on the different types of presentations of the skin disease throughout Leviticus 13. Let me be clear here. *Leprosy* would be a disease included in *tzara'at,* but it is not the *only* disease. So, where did the translation of leprosy come from in this passage?

In the 3rd century BC, the Hebrew Scriptures were translated into the Greek Septuagint. When they made it to Leviticus 13, they used the base word for leprosy to translate *tzara'at.* Later, Latin translators transliterated the Greek word they chose to translate it using their word *lepra.*

Now, we know that *leprosy* was around as far back as 600 BC. We have reports of it in India, China, and Egypt. The problem is that there is not really any evidence that points to it being in Israel at the time of Leviticus. Obviously, we do see it in the New Testament. We will talk about that more in a few minutes. By the way, does anybody know what *leprosy* is called today? Hansen's disease. It is a bacterial disease. The bacteria attack the peripheral nervous system (outside brain and spinal cord) and they develop a loss of pain in their nerves. Again, it is important for us to understand Hansen's disease, especially as we talk about some of the lepers of the New Testament. Hold that thought for now.

This term of *tzara'at* in Leviticus 13 is much more all-encompassing. We see several types of skin infections that fall into the category. Verses 1-8 talk about *skin eruptions.* If a person developed a *swelling, rash, or bright spot,* he would be taken to the priest to be examined. We know from Jewish records that priests were looking for two of the three symptoms. If the hair on the skin had turned white and the sore was below the surface of the skin, the person is declared ceremonially unclean. If it wasn't below the surface of the skin and the hair had not turned white, they were isolated for seven days and then reexamined. Basically, if it spread at all by that point, they were declared unclean.

We see quite a few accounts in the Old Testament that fall in this category. In Exodus 4, God is showing Moses His power. He instructs Moses to put his hand in his bosom. Then, God tells him to pull it out. What did his hand look like? *Leprous like snow* (Ex. 4:6). In Numbers 12, we read the story of Miriam, Moses' sister. As she is speaking out against her brother, the Lord gave her *leprosy* or *tzara'at*

(Numbers 12:10). In 2 Kings 5, we see both Naaman and Gehazi have *leprosy*. 2 Chronicles 26 tells of an incident with King Uzziah where was struck with *leprosy* after entering the Temple to burn incense and being corrected by the priests. Now, all of these examples are just one type of *tzara'at*.

Verses 9-17 discuss *chronic skin disease* as a diagnosis of *tzara'at*. White hair and raw flesh in the swelling is the characteristic that the priest was looking for. Next, verses 18-23 talk about *boils* as the cause of *tzara'at*. Job was afflicted with boils. The ten plagues included boils. These are examples of *tzara'at*.

Verses 24-28 talk about *burns*. Verses 29-37 talk about *sores on the head or chin*. Verses 38-39 talk about *white spots on the skin*. Verses 40-44 talk about *baldness*.

I just wanted you to get this picture of how many things the term *leprosy* or *tzara'at* covers in Leviticus 13. Over the years, rabbis began to identify specific skin diseases that fall in the *leprosy* family. Some listed as many as **seventy-two** different diseases. They used the example of Miriam in Numbers 12 to teach that **gossip** or **slander** is what caused her *leprosy*. It was an *outward* sign of an *inward* problem. Therefore, they said that you better always watch your words very carefully. You better not commit *lashon hara* (speaking evil of other people). Another thing you may not know is that among the sixty-one defilements of ancient Jewish laws, leprosy was second only to a dead body in seriousness. What does God say that a person is to do if he or she has *leprosy*?

> *As for the leper who has the infection, his clothes shall be torn, and the hair of his head shall be uncovered, and he shall cover his mustache and cry, "Unclean! Unclean!" He shall remain unclean all the days during which he has the infection; he is unclean. He shall live alone; his dwelling shall be outside the camp.*
> **Leviticus 13:45-46**

It's that time a year in my pediatric office. *Rash season.* I have been seeing a lot of rashes over the past month and a half. Before the kids finished school, I would often have parents bring their child in because the schools require a note saying that the child isn't contagious before they are able to return. Without a note, the children are not welcome to come back. In essence, they are *kicked out* until they have a note stating they are healthy.

Leviticus 13 teaches that it was the **priest's** job to diagnose and separate those with leprosy.

If the priest diagnosed a person with leprosy, what did that person have to do?

The leper had to *tear his clothes, uncover his head*, and *cover his mustache*. Sometimes, we read passages in the Old Testament and think, "That is crazy. Why would God have them do something like that?" These specific actions were *signs of mourning.* If someone walking down the street had torn clothes, an uncovered head, and their hand over their mouth, it was a sign that that person was **mourning** over a loss.

To top it off, the leper had to shout "Unclean! Unclean!" as they walked down the road. Can you imagine the absolute humiliation? If someone was diagnosed with leprosy, that person's entire life was turned upside down!

If all of that wasn't bad enough, a leper was also **cast out of camp** to live *alone*. Away from his wife. Away from his kids. Away from his friends. Away from his job. Away from everything he has ever known.

In your mind, fast-forward about 1400 years. It is the time of Jesus. Things have changed in Israel. *Leprosy* (what we call Hansen's disease today) is in full force. Jesus and His disciples are in Galilee. He is busy preaching in synagogues and casting out demons. Then, a leper comes into his path. Now, you have to picture this man. He is absolutely despised. Others look at him thinking *his* sin caused leprosy. He has been kicked out of the community. Because of the laws of the day, this man wasn't allowed to come within six feet of any other human. He wasn't allowed to come within 150 feet of anyone if the wind was blowing. Do you see him? Now, let me give you a description of a leper:

> "The hair falls from the head and eye-brows; the nails loosen, decay and drop off; joint after joint of the fingers and toes shrink up and slowly fall away. The gums are absorbed, and the teeth disappear. The nose, the eyes, the tongue and the palate are slowly consumed."

Do you see this man?

Read Mark 1:40-45.

This man is begging for healing because he has nowhere else to turn. The text says that Jesus was **moved with compassion**. This Greek word for *compassion* is the most intense word in the Greek language used for emotion. It is a deep-down gut-level type of compassion. It is the compassion a parent has for a child when the child is going through a hard time. Then, what did Jesus do? He stretched out His hand and **touched** him. This man hadn't been touched in *years*, and our Savior *touched* him. And he was cleansed. Jesus told him to go to the priest and fulfill Leviticus 13 and 14.

As I have been thinking about the horrible disease of leprosy, I am left with this thought: God *blessed us* with leprosy. That sounds like an absolutely ridiculous statement. But, hang with me. Leprosy is *gross*. Leprosy is *painful*. Leprosy *separates* the leper from the clean. Do you see a correlation with sin? Sin is *gross*. Sin is *painful*. Sin *separates* us from a Holy God.

Leprosy was cast away and dealt with harshly. In the very same way, sin must be cast away and dealt with harshly!

Think about those kids that come into my office for a note for school. They need something declaring that they are *clean*. They need something saying that they are *healthy*. In the very same way, each of us needs someone that declares us *clean*. We don't have to go to an earthly priest today for that note. Hebrews 4 says that we have a Great High Priest who is able to give *mercy* and *grace*. We have a Great High Priest who is able to *cleanse* and *heal*. See, leprosy is a picture of how seriously God wanted to deal with sin. That nasty picture you had in your mind of the man with leprosy as I asked you to imagine him is a picture of how *we* look spiritually without Christ! And when we come to Him, He is moved with compassion. And He touches us. And He heals us. And He declares us clean.

God is *still* in the healing business today. He still gives clean bills of health to those who ask for it. Understand what happens when someone accepts Jesus. It is just as big of a miracle as when God touched that leper in Mark 1 and healed him from his physical deformities.

My Life as a Wave Offering

Before we get into the details of Leviticus 14, I want us to get back into an account that we read about in the New Testament. We talked about it as we discussed chapter 13. Now, get there with me.

He hadn't seen his family since the diagnosis. He hadn't been touched in years. But the day came when he saw Him. Jesus. The One they called the Messiah. The One who had healed Simon's mother-in-law. The One who had healed many with sickness in Judea. The One who had the power to cast out demons.

Leper*: "Lord, if You are willing, You can make me clean."*

Amazingly, Jesus begins to reach out His hand. The man who hadn't been touched since the day he had been cast out was touched by the Son of God.

Jesus*: "I am willing; be cleansed."*

Immediately, the leprosy was gone!

Jesus*: "Go and show yourself to the **priest** and make an **offering** for your **cleansing**, just **as Moses commanded**, as a testimony to them."*

* * * * * * * *

The account of Jesus healing the leper found in Mark 1 and Luke 5 is incredible. Leprosy was a disease that was *not* curable. If a person was diagnosed with leprosy, it was a hopeless situation. They would no longer be a part of society. Their life was changed forever.

But let me tell you about an amazing day as a leper met Jesus Christ. He *begged* Jesus for healing. Wouldn't you do the same? You see, there was no other hope. Jesus was his *only* hope of healing from leprosy. And Jesus was *moved with compassion* (Mark 1:41) as He healed the leper.

Then, He told this man to go show the priest and make an offering just as Moses commanded. That command is found in Leviticus 14. Today, we are going to look at what a person with *tzara'at* was to do to be cleansed and re-established into the community.

Read **Leviticus 14:1-2a**.

Instead of reading all the details of Leviticus 14, let's just discuss the *three stages* involved in verses 3 through 20.

Stage 1 (verses 3-7) – Location: **Outside of camp**. The priest examines the person with *tzara'at*. Why would this take place *outside* the camp? The person is still unclean. He hasn't been pronounced clean at this point. The priest must come out to meet him. If the priest sees that the person is free from the *tzara'at*, there is an elaborate ritual that must take place.

Look at **verse 4**. They needed two live clean birds, cedar wood, scarlet string, and hyssop. Does anybody know what is significant about the cedar wood, scarlet string, and hyssop? Last week, we said that there were **61** defilements listed in Jewish law. Of those 61, only **one** was considered more serious. Do you remember what it was? **Death.** Do you know the *only* other time cedar wood, scarlet string, and hyssop are used together in the Bible? **Numbers 19** – They are used for purification of someone who touches a dead body. *These three elements show us the seriousness of tzara'at!*

The priest takes the two birds and kills one of them over a vessel of living water (*mayim chaim*). Living water means water from a stream or a well that has not been standing or touched by human hands. It is water that is full of *life*. One of the birds is killed and its blood goes into this living water. The priest dips they hyssop (which acts like a sponge) into the blood and sprinkles the healed person seven times. The second bird is released in the open field. Rabbis taught that the free bird carries off the impurity of the person.

Stage 2 (verses 8-9) – Location: **May enter camp**. After this ceremony, the healed person must wash his clothes, shave his hair, and bathe himself. Why was *shaving* a big deal? If you see an orthodox Jew today, you will notice that he often has a long beard and these long sideburns. They look weird. Men don't cut them. Why? God's Word says, "*Do not cut the hair at the sides of your head or clip off the edges of your beard" (Lev 19:27).* Today, these long sideburns are called *payot*. However, God wants those who have a skin disease to do a thorough washing and shaving as a symbol that all impurity has been removed that this person is starting new. He is clean. At this point, he may enter camp, but he has to stay outside his tent for seven days. Then, on the seventh day, he shaves again. He shaves his hair, his beard, his eyebrows, and all other hair on his body. He washes his clothes and bathes once again and is considered *clean*.

Stage 3 (verses 10-20) – Location: **Tent of Meeting.** In these verses, the person who has been healed was to provide several offerings: a *grain* offering, a *guilt* offering, a *wave* offering, and *sin* offering, and a *burnt* offering. Let's think of *why* God would instruct each of these offerings. Why would He want a **grain** offering? This is the offering found in Leviticus 2 that you give to God in *every* scene of life. It is a *personalized* offering. There were four types: no heat, low heat, high heat, or scorching. The way you cook your grain offering depends on if everything is going great (no heat) or if you are in the middle of the fire (deep-fried). So, this grain offering is saying to God, "*Everything You do is spot on! Even though we have been away from Your people due to our skin disease, we trust You, Lord."*

Next was a **guilt** offering. We talked about this in Leviticus 5. Why do you think God wanted His people to give a guilt offering in this ceremony? It is a payment for *sin*. But, was the cause of their skin disease *sin*? Well, we talked about multiple examples in which God gave *tzara'at* to people who had sinned in chapter 13. Remember Miriam in Numbers 12? She spoke against Moses and God gave her *tzara'at*. So, some people say a guilt offering was offered in case their skin disease was due to disobedience. It is an offering of, "*let me just cover all of my basis.*" It is kind of like me and baptism. I was sprinkled as a baby. I was sprinkled as a teenager. And I was immersed here. I have covered all my basis as far as baptism! But this is not really the accepted thought of *why* God wanted a guilt offering. See, if a person was away from the tabernacle, he is no longer serving the Lord. So scholars say that they offered a guilt offering to compensate God for loss of service to Him. Listen to me. Do you understand that this church is not just a place for you to come to hear Sunday school lessons and sermons? It breaks my heart to see people not plugged in because they view the church as just a place to come to hear a sermon. **You were created to serve!** God put you here in this church and gave you the gifts He gave you for a reason. You are to *use them*. See, a person with a skin disease had to pay a **guilt offering** because they weren't using their gifts during the time they were separated from the camp. Today, if guilt offerings were still required due to lack of service, would you need to bring Him a guilt offering to make restitution for not using your gifts for Him?

A **sin** offering was given in these verses. That was Leviticus 4. Why did people give sin offerings? They were for *unintentional sins*. A **burnt** offering was also given (Leviticus 1).

Now, I want to go back to an offering listed in verse 12. We have briefly discussed this offering in the past, but I want to make sure you understand the importance of this offering.

> *Then the priest shall take the one male lamb and bring it for a guilt offering, with the log of oil, and present them as a wave offering before the LORD.*
> **Leviticus 14:12**

What is a *wave* offering? We discussed it in Leviticus 8. A wave offering involved the priest taking the breast of the animal and waving it back and forth to make a sincere petition in true worship. *It expressed thankfulness and commitment to God.* But it also served another purpose: **A wave offering was given to recognize <u>total dependence</u> on God.**

Why did this person need to give a *wave offering*? Because he had **no hope** of being healed without Jesus!

*Today, Jesus remains the only true healer. As I think about that day that Jesus healed the leper, I am struck by His compassion. The same compassion He had when He was placed on the cross for my sins. The same compassion He had the day He saved me. My question: **Is my life a wave offering in return for His compassion?** Do I* *recognize my **total dependence** on Him? I had no hope of healing myself. My entire life must be an offering to Him.*

Now, I want us to close by thinking about one last thing mentioned about the guilt offering. Look at **verse 14**. Some of the blood was put on the lobe of the right ear. Some of the blood was put on the thumb of the right hand. Some of the blood was put on the big toe on the right foot. What on earth is that about? Again, it goes back to the **consecration** of the priests in Leviticus 8. It is a ceremony saying that this person with the skin disease from that day forward would be **all in** for the Lord. Their ear (**head**) was to be consecrated for two reasons. One, it was part of the head (so their thoughts would be on the Lord) *and* their ear was to be in tune with His voice. Their thumb (**hands**) were to be consecrated so that their actions would match the Lord's instructions. Their toe (**feet**) were to be consecrated so that their walk would always match His and they would go and the Lord led them. It was the same for this person that had the skin disease. And it is the same for us!

God still calls us to have a life in which our *thoughts* are on Him, our *ear* is in tune with His voice, our *hands* are busy doing what He instructs us to do, and our *feet* are busy going where He leads us.

*Just as there was a need for **guilt** offerings for those who were not serving the Lord due to their separation, you may need to bring Him a **guilt** offering today because you have not been using the spiritual gifts He has entrusted to you. Or maybe you haven't been looking for ways to serve Him. Or maybe you just haven't been an active part of a church body. Do you realize that **each** of you is a part of the Lord's **body**? If you are not being active in a church body or you are not using your gifts, you are **hampering** Christ. If any part of my body is not functioning, my body is hampered. The same is true for Christ's body. Understand you are a vital part of what He wants to do. You have unique gifts that are set up for exactly what He wants to accomplish through you. Do you need to bring a **guilt** offering to Him today because you haven't been faithful in using those gifts?*

*You may need to offer Him a **wave** offering, maybe for the first time in your life. Can I be honest? We often live lives that don't **need** the Lord. We don't really **total depend** on Him! We have money in our bank accounts. We have food in our fridge. We are blessed. And we **never** give Him wave offerings because we don't realize how much we need Him. Maybe today your offering is a realization that you absolutely **cannot** do anything for His kingdom without **Him**.*

*Lastly, you may know that you are not truly **all in** for the Lord. Your head, hands, and feet are not really His. You are being selfish in your walk and you know it. Let Him mold you into who He created you to be.*

A Clean Tabernacle

Turn to **Leviticus 15**. Today, we are going to talk about a very exciting topic: *bodily discharges*. Let's take a quick overview of the chapter. Verses 2-15 talk about abnormal bodily discharges in men (things like gonorrhea). Verses 16-18 discuss normal discharges of men. Verses 19-24 focus on normal discharges of women. Finally, verses 25-30 talk about abnormal discharges of women.

Abnormal bodily discharges of men (vv. 2-15) – The man was unclean and anything he touched became unclean. Anyone that touched him became unclean. He had to wash his clothes and bathe in water. Once the discharge was healed, he washed his clothes and bathed again and waited seven days. On the eighth day, he offered two doves or two pigeons to the priest. One was a *sin* offering and the other was a *burnt* offering. These provided atonement for the man.

Normal discharges of men (vv. 16-18) – Any emission of semen for any reason made a man unclean for the rest of the day. Now, *why* do you think God gave this law? I will never forget going to Caesarea Philippi in Israel. Do you remember what we said pagans there at Caesarea Philippi thought would cause fertility for their families and their crops? Sexual activity. Men with women. Women with women. Men with men. People with animals. It was *gross*. They believed this is what caused the gods to have sex, and when they had sex, they would get rain. God, on the other hand, said that sex causes His people to be *unclean*. It makes them unfit for worship in the Tabernacle. He didn't want his people to go anywhere near those pagan practices.

Another thought about this. Did God want His people to intermarry with people of other religions? No! Deuteronomy 7:3-4 says,

> *"Furthermore, you shall not intermarry with them; you shall not give your daughters to their sons, nor shall you take their daughters for your sons. For they will turn your sons away from following Me to serve other gods; then the anger of the LORD will be kindled against you and He will quickly destroy you."*

There are warnings not to marry pagans in Exodus, Joshua, Judges, 1 Kings, and Ezra. With the type of regulations we see listed in Leviticus 15, do you think it would be a deterrent for people of religions to *want* to marry a Jew? It absolutely was!

Normal discharges of women (vv. 19-24) – During menstruation, a woman was impure for seven days. Whatever she touched curing these seven days became unclean. If she touched a chair and then her husband sat in it, he would be unclean until the end of the day. Jewish law says that at the end of the seven days, a woman must bathe to be clean. There is a Biblical story that involves this law. The story of David and Bathsheba in 2 Samuel 11. David looks down from his house and sees Bathsheba bathing on her roof. Now, the Hebrew word used is *not* a word used for just a normal bath because she is dirty. It is a *ceremonial washing*. The kind a woman does after her period. Another thing you might need to know. God designed it where women washed at *peak* times in their cycle. She was primed to get pregnant at that moment. It wasn't a surprise that she became pregnant during that encounter.

Now, there is something else about menstruation. Did you know that the Hebrew word for menstruation used in Leviticus 15 (*niddâ*) is later used as a metaphor to describe Israel's sins?

> **2 Chronicles 29:11** – "*Then he (Hezekiah) said to them, 'Listen to me, O Levites. Consecrate yourselves now, and consecrate the house of the* LORD*, the God of your fathers, and carry the uncleanness* (**niddâ**) *out from the holy place.'* "

> **Ezra 9:10-11** – "*Now, our God, what shall we say after this? For we have forsaken Your commandments, which You have commanded by Your servants the prophets, saying, 'The land which you are entering to possess is an unclean* (**niddâ**) *land with the uncleanness* (**niddâ**) *of the peoples of the lands, with their abominations which have filled it from end to end and with their impurity.'* "

> **Ezekiel 36:17** - "*Son of man, when the house of Israel was living in their own land, they defiled it by their ways and their deeds; their way before Me was like the uncleanness of a woman in her impurity* (**niddâ**)."

> **Zechariah 13:1** – "*In that day a fountain will be opened for the house of David and for the inhabitants of Jerusalem, for sin and for impurity* (**niddâ**)."

I hope you are getting this picture. Just like a woman's menstruation made her *unclean* and *unable to serve the Lord*, God then says that **Israel's sins** made them *unclean* and *unable to serve Him*. You know, I have noticed something at my office. I work with a ton of women. If I ever go to the bathroom, more often than not, there are empty wrappers of feminine pads in the trash. As a man, I have no idea how women deal with that stuff every month! Did you know that Jewish man prays this prayer every single day: ***"Blessed are you, LORD our God, Ruler of the Universe, who has not made me a woman."*** Let me tell you, that is not because they view women as *inferior*. Actually, Jewish men realize that they don't have the pain tolerance to go through everything women deal with. Therefore, they praise God that He created them as a male. Now, I think most men would agree that menstrual cycles are pretty gross. Right? Do you realize that God views our **sin** the very same way? Don't take your sin lightly. View it the same way God views it!

Abnormal discharges of women (vv. 25-30) – If a woman had a discharge not related to menstruation, anything she touched while having the discharge was unclean. Whoever she touched became unclean. When the discharge went away, she had to wait seven days before she could be ceremonially clean. On the eighth day, she gave two doves or two pigeons to the priest as a *sin* offering and a *burnt* offering. It is *this* context that we find a story in the New Testament. Think about this with me.

> *The woman traveled 30 miles to see Him. The whole time, she thought to herself, "If I can just touch His clothes, I will be healed" (Mark 5:28). The bleeding had been going on for* **12 years**. *12 years of being* **unclean** *due to the Law of Leviticus 15. 12 years of having no physical contact with* **anyone**. *12 years of being* **sick** *and* **unaccepted in society**.

> *She had tried to find healing in the past. In fact, she has spent every dime she had looking for a physician to heal her (Mark 5:26). But the amazing part about the entire story is that, while her body failed her, one thing remained very strong:* **her faith**. *That is why she traveled 30 miles to meet Jesus.*

> *When she saw Him in that crowd, she approached Him and touched His cloak (Mark 5:27). According to Leviticus 15:19, a simple touch of Jesus by a woman in her condition* **should have** *made Him unclean. But it didn't! Instead, the opposite happened.* **Immediately, her bleeding stopped** *(Mark 5:29). At that moment, her healthy faith in the Son of God made her unhealthy body healthy once again. This is* **grace**. *This is* **Jesus**.

God tells us in Leviticus 15 that any bodily discharge makes a person *unclean*. Not only that but any person that touches a person having the discharge also becomes *unclean*. It was a serious business.

> ***Thus you shall keep the sons of Israel separated from their uncleanness, so that they will not die in their uncleanness by their defiling My tabernacle that is among them.***
> **Leviticus 15:31**

According to this text, what would happen if a person came into the tabernacle while being unclean? **His tabernacle would become defiled.** This word means that His tabernacle would be *unsuitable for communing with a Holy God*. I am guessing that the Jews took this law very seriously! One person's disobedience could defile the entire tabernacle, rendering communion with God impossible.

We have become His tabernacle (1 Corinthians 6:19-20). He lives inside *me* and *you*. News flash: He wants *His tabernacle* to be **pure**. He wants no part in sharing His living quarters with that which is *unclean*. In my life, what are the things that are defiling His tabernacle? What are the things that must be removed so that I may have a tabernacle suitable for communing with a Holy God? What are the things that you need to remove today?

Now, you may say, "That is impossible. It is impossible to live a life suitable for communing with a Holy God. Our flesh will always defile our bodies." And to that, I say, "You are absolutely correct." Which is why I love the story of the bleeding woman who touched Jesus in Mark 5. Can you imagine her boldness? **According to Leviticus 15, the moment she touched Jesus, He *should have* become unfit for use!** That was what the law declared. But this was *Jesus.* And He was about to show the world the **grace** that only He can provide. *By His grace, she was healed.* At that moment, Jesus was making the statement that *every person*, no matter the condition, may be healed and used for His service.

*The same is true for me. Did you know that when the God of the Universe looks at me, He does not even **see** my sins? The blood of Jesus has paid for each and every sin that I have ever committed. God, Himself, says that He doesn't remember our sins (Isaiah 43:25, Hebrews 8:12, Hebrews 10:17). I am so thankful for His **grace** that covers my filth. Just like the bleeding woman, by His grace, He has made me **clean** and useful for His kingdom!*

There are two sides to sin coin today. We must view sin the way God does. We have an enemy that wants to deceive us into thinking sin is no big deal. God says, "It is gross!" He longs for a *spotless bride.* He longs for a people who want to please Him in everything. He wants us to take sin seriously because of the seriousness of our sin. Jesus **died** because of our sin. How dare we take sin lightly? Today, there may be sin in your life that you have been brushing off. You haven't dealt with it. It is time to purify God's temple. It is time to give Him a place to live in us *suitable* for His holy nature.

Thankfully, the other side of the coin is the incredible grace of God. While we cannot clean ourselves up enough to be completely pure, God can touch us and make us pure. Can I tell you a secret? God loves to cleanse and redeem His people. He is a redeeming God who longs to restore us into the men and women He has created us to be. Once He purifies us, He says, "*It is as if you have never sinned.*" But we have an enemy that wants to whisper lies in our ears – *"You aren't good enough." "Don't you remember how you have constantly let God down?" "He can never use you. Remember your past?" "Nobody will listen to you because of what you have done in the past."* And God looks at us and says, "*I have made you clean. I have redeemed you. I have restored you. It is as if you have never sinned.*"

Listen, don't let the enemy convince you that God cannot use you for the kingdom.

Examining the Scapegoat

Today, we will be in Leviticus 16. In English, the topic we are studying is the Day of Atonement. What is the Hebrew name? *Yom Kippur.* I want us to begin with just a quick overview of Yom Kippur. First of all, why would there need to be a Day of Atonement? I mean, we discussed all of the offerings already. Why is the Day of Atonement even necessary? Well, do you think *every* Israelite was diligent about atoning for their sin? Do you think the process was always carried out exactly as prescribed? No. These are humans. They mess things up. They don't always offer sacrifices when they are supposed to. So, God sets aside a day for purifying the Holy of Holies, the Holy Place, and the entire Tabernacle once a year. And, in the process, the *people* are also made clean. See, the people walk away from the Day of Atonement and *know* they **all is forgiven**. They were *clean* (v. 30). By the way, if you back up a verse, you also see that God gave them a specific day to celebrate Yom Kippur every year (tenth day of the seventh month – v. 29).

Before we dig in, I want you to understand how big Yom Kippur is to a Jew, especially to an ancient Jew. It was the **most important** Jewish holiday. So much so, we see in the literature that they simply referred to Yom Kippur as "The Day." Yom Kippur is always after **Rosh Hashanah** (The Feast of Trumpets). Do you know how many days are between Rosh Hashanah and Yom Kippur? **10 days**. These days are very important. We will talk about these days in a future lesson. I want us to put all of the Jewish holidays together so that you will see how Jesus has truly fulfilled almost every Jewish holiday. It will knock your socks off. So, stay tuned for that. But know that the Day of Atonement is incredibly important to a Jew.

Look at **verse 1**. What has just happened when God gave the instructions of Yom Kippur? *Aaron's 2 sons have just died.* Does anybody remember that story? **Leviticus 10:1-2**. Nabab and Abihu were Aaron's two oldest sons. God had just shown up among them (Leviticus 9:23) and the *first thing* these two men did were to offer **strange fire** before the Lord. They gave Him the offering *they* wanted to give, not the offering that *He* wanted them to give. What did God do to them? He killed them.

Leviticus 16:2 – Aaron's two sons have just died, and Moses was to tell Aaron that he can't enter the Holy of Holies anytime he wants, or he will die, just like his sons.

Think about the sacrifice. What animals does Aaron need for Yom Kippur? We see in verse 3 that a **bull (sin offering)** and a **ram (burnt offering)** were needed. These were brought to the Tabernacle by Aaron. What else does he need? In verse 5, we read that he needs **two male goats (sin offering)** and a **ram (burnt offering)**. These were taken from the people. Now, Aaron must make atonement for himself with the bull (we will get to that in a second) but notice that he does something unusual with the two goats. **Read verses 7-10**. Aaron was to *cast lots* to determine which goat represented God and which represented the scapegoat. Again, the idea of casting lots is all over the place in the Bible (including the New

Testament). The goat that represented God was given as a **sin offering** while the goat that represented the scapegoat was released into the wilderness. I want us to dive into this in more detail in a few minutes.

Next, Aaron offered the bull that he brought for a **sin offering** for himself and his household (remember what his sons just did!) **Read verses 12-13**. What is this about? Why would there need to be a *cloud of incense* over the mercy seat?

> **Exodus 33:20** – "He [God] said, "you **cannot see my face**, for man shall not see me and live.'"

> **1 Timothy 6:15–17** – "He who is the blessed and only Sovereign, the King of kings and Lord of lords, who alone has immortality, who dwells in unapproachable light, whom **no one has ever seen or can see**. To him be honor and eternal dominion."

> **1 John 4:12** – "**No one has ever seen God**; if we love one another, God abides in us."

Where did God meet with the high priest? Specifically, it says that He meets with them "above the mercy seat, from between the two cherubim which are upon the ark of the testimony" (Exodus 25:22). So, there needed to be a cloud of smoke over the mercy seat so that Aaron (or the high priest) would not *see* Him. Can you imagine how nervous Aaron must have been to enter the Holy of Holies? What if he didn't do something right? He was a dead man!

Next, Aaron was to sprinkle some of the blood of the bull that he had offered on the mercy seat and in front of the mercy seat. Then, he leaves the Holy of Holies and slaughters the goat of the sin offering. He brings it back into the Holy of Holies. By the way, many of you know that Jews **never** say God's name, right? They **never** say "Yahweh." They don't want to take a chance in *profaning* His name. They don't want to take a chance of using His name casually. So, they don't say it. Well, there was **one** exception. On Yom Kippur, when the High Priest would enter the Holy of Holies with the blood from the goat, he would say His name – Yahweh. This was the *only* time, and the High Priest was the *only* person who would **ever** say the name of God. They only other time the High Priest would say the name would be to tell his successor how to pronounce God's name in his dying breath. So, Aaron comes back in and sprinkles the goat's blood on the mercy seat as well. After that, he goes back out to the altar to make atonement there. He puts the blood of both the bull and the goat on the horns. This is for the Israelite's sin.

What about the scapegoat? **Read verses 21-22**. Aaron lays his hands on this scapegoat and confesses all of Israel's sins. It is as if he is putting all of their sins on the head of the goat. Then, it is released into the wilderness. Again, we will come back to this in a moment.

Aaron goes into the Holy Place, takes off his clothes and leaves them there. He bathes, puts on fresh clothes, and offers the two rams for burnt offerings (one for him and one for the people).

*Now, when we read about the **scapegoat** in Leviticus 16, who does that represent?*

I want you to remember that the high priest would cast lots to determine which goat represented **the Lord** and which would be the **scapegoat** (v. 8).

I have always been taught that the scapegoat represented Jesus. After all, He bore all of our sins. So, He is our scapegoat, right? What if I told you that there is a mountain of evidence that disagrees with that stance? Now, I am not trying to upset anyone, but I want to show you some things that have really challenged my views on the scapegoat. Let me be clear – I am *not* saying that the scapegoat doesn't represent Jesus, but I want to examine this from another point of view. It is like being in school and the teacher makes you defend a position that you don't agree with just to understand that side of the equation. Well, let's just take a look today and see what we think about the scapegoat when we get finished looking at the other side of the equation. So many times in church, we are taught something and we never really examine it in great detail. We just accept it as truth. I don't want to do that today. I want us to really look at this critically and see what conclusion we come to. FACTS:

1. The word "scapegoat" was invented by William Tyndale in his 1530 English translation of the Bible. Does anybody's Bible translate it with a different word? The actual Hebrew word used is **Azazel**. More on this in a few minutes.

2. The scapegoat took on the sins of the people but was *set free* in the wilderness. The scapegoat was *not* a sin offering. The scapegoat was *not* slain. If the scapegoat represented Jesus, why would the law call for the scapegoat to roam free in the *wilderness*? Over and over in the Bible, the wilderness is synonymous with *evil*. This seems odd.

3. The **scapegoat** and **the Lord** stood in *opposition* as the high priest cast lots for each (v. 8). It specifically says that one lot was **for** the Lord while the other was **for** the scapegoat (Azazel). Would something that represents Jesus stand in opposition to the Lord?

4. Biblically, a *goat* usually represents *evil*. Jesus compared His followers to **sheep**, but those who did evil to **goats** (Matthew 25:32-46). Even in the Old Testament, God says that He would *punish* goats (Zechariah 10:3). Would a *goat* represent Jesus? It's worth asking.

5. Jewish records tell us how the ceremony was actually performed with the scapegoat. Initially, the goat was taken 10 miles outside of the camp. They said that the wilderness was **evil** and the scapegoat was carrying

the sin to where he belongs. The sin would no longer be at the Tabernacle. But what if someone came in contact with the scapegoat in the wilderness? How would you know it was the scapegoat? Or, what if the scapegoat made its way back to camp? How would you know it was the scapegoat? So, they began to do something to make sure everyone knew that it was the scapegoat. They would tie a scarlet cloth around his head. Jewish tradition says that *if* God accepted the sacrifice, the scarlet cloth would turn white. If He did not accept the sacrifice, it would stay red and all Israel would stay in mourning for the next year.

As time went on, there is one documented occasion when the scapegoat returned to Jerusalem after he was set free. They altered the ceremony. They began to carry the scapegoat to a specific place in the wilderness where there was a steep cliff with jagged rocks below. They led the scapegoat with a red string that would turn white if God was pleased with the Israelites. When the goat was *released* at that steep cliff, it was released to die. See, the Jews viewed the scapegoat as **evil.** They never wanted the scapegoat to return back to the camp. If the scapegoat represented Jesus, why would they have understood the scapegoat to be *evil?*

One interesting tidbit about the red string/white string thing. Jewish records say that the string **never** turned white when leading the scapegoat to its death for the **40 years** leading up to the destruction of the Temple. When was the destruction of the Temple? *70 AD.* Subtract 40 years. Does anything happen around **30 A.D.** of significance? At the time of Jesus' death, God says, "I am not accepting the scapegoat as a sacrifice anymore." That's pretty cool.

6. The Book of Enoch is quoted by Jude (Jude 1:14-15). During the time of Jesus' ministry, the Book of Enoch was apparently widely known. **Azazel** (later translated *scapegoat*) was specifically defined as a name for **Satan** in the Book of Enoch. Not only that, *all sin* was ascribed to **Azazel (Satan)**. The Book of Enoch specifically states that **Azazel** was to be taken to the desert and placed on "jagged rocks." This sounds very much like how the Jews actually performed this ceremony.

So, why is all of this even important? I was reading 1 John2 last week which says,

> *"As for you, the anointing which you received from Him abides in you, and you have no need for anyone to teach you; but as His anointing teaches you about all things, and is true and is not a lie, and just as it has taught you, you abide in Him" (v. 27).*

How often do we really rely on the Holy Spirit to teach us and how often do we just accept what we have always been taught by others to be the truth? Let me ask you a direct question - Are you digging into His Word? At the end of 2 Peter, Peter finishes his letter by pleading that followers of Christ not just accept the teachings of others, but to **diligently** dig into His Word and **grow** in Him. Are you doing that? Are you so consumed with wanting to know the truth that you want to understand the *context* of His Word? With each of these lessons, I am trying to bring out context to the Word. Doesn't it make it come alive? Listen, if you need help with resources, I can share with you some of the resources I use. But it takes a heart that is **longing** for truth. It takes a heart that is **diligent** and knows that it takes **time** to truly dig deep and find the truth. These lessons take a long time to get together, but how rewarding is it when God opens our eyes to truth because we are willing to dig?

I don't know for sure if **Azazel** represents Jesus. I know that is what I have always been taught. But, at the end of the day, I am thankful that the **atonement** has been made. You see, I kind of think the sin offering made **to the Lord** in the story is more of a picture of Jesus. It was spotless. It was chosen by God. And it was slain for the forgiveness of sins. *That* is a picture of Jesus. I challenge you to wrestle with God's Word. I promise that it is in the moments of wrestling with Him that you will be molded into the man or woman that He desires.

A Blood Covering

Leviticus 17 marks a shift in theme. The first 16 chapters of Leviticus can be summarized by one word: **atonement**. We have discussed in detail all of the types of offerings made for atonement. Primarily, these chapters deal with the issue of having a proper relationship with God. They instructed Israel how to love God with all its soul, mind and strength. However, there is a change in focus as we reach chapter 17 and following. These chapters deal with how the people were to remain in fellowship with their brother. Essentially, chapters 17-26 provide a commentary on how to live out the Golden Rule, "You shall love your neighbor as yourself." The theme of these chapters shifts from **atonement** to **holiness**. Scholars call Leviticus 17-26 the "Holiness Code." If you remember way back when we began talking about Leviticus, I told you that Leviticus is the first book taught to young Jew children. Why? It dealt with two things – how to worship God AND how to be **holy**. For the rest of our study of Leviticus, we will really focus on the *holiness* aspect.

So, let's get going with Leviticus 17. There are several laws that we will cover today, and, towards the end of our time, we will look at how Leviticus 17 relates to the life of Jesus.

Read verses 1-9. The text says the ox or lamb or goat that is slaughtered must be brought to the doorway of the tent of meeting. What offering are we talking about here? **Peace offering**. This was Leviticus 3. It is also called a **fellowship offering**. Does anybody remember much about this offering? This is the *only* offering in which the worshipper joins in the meal. Do you remember? We aren't going to get into all the specifics, but we discussed that there were three types of peace offerings. The worshipper gave God the blood and the choicest parts of the animal. And then, they sit down and have a meal *with* God. This is the type of offering we are discussing here in Leviticus 17.

Now, I want you to think about something. Before the flood, was it okay to kill and eat an animal? Well, Genesis 1 teaches that God considers animals *good* and that He created *plants* for food. As a matter of fact, the end of Genesis 1 says that the plants were to be food for the animals as well. Then we get to Genesis 9. After the flood, God changes the rules. **Genesis 9:3-4**. Now, Jews teach that, once the Tabernacle was erected, God changes the rules yet again. They say that He makes sheep and cattle *only* for **peace offerings** at this point. They are no longer food for any reason. They use Leviticus 17 as their source for this explanation. But Christian scholars have traditionally taught this a different way. Let's consider a scenario.

I am an Israelite living at this time period. Let's say that a sheep is born. Can *any* sheep be used for sacrifice? **No**. Animals used for sacrifice had to be *without blemish*, right? So, do you think most animals born would fit into the category of being able to be used for sacrifice or do you think most animals born would fit into the category of blemished? Now, I don't have sheep, but from what I read, upon careful examination, they would find something on most animals that they would consider a blemish and say that they were not fit for sacrifice. Therefore, there were two sets of animals. Those that were *consecrated* (set aside to be used in sacrifice to God) and those that were *not*. Leviticus 17 is only talking about the animals that were consecrated, not the other animals.

Why is any of this important? We must understand the emphasis of Leviticus 17. There were people slaughtering *consecrated* animals in the "open field" (not at the Tabernacle). These animals should have been a sacrifice to God, but they were being used for other purposes. One of the things we discussed in Leviticus 16 was the idea that the *wilderness* (or the area around the Tabernacle) was considered *evil*. A goat was sent *into* the wilderness to carry the sins of the people away from the Tabernacle once a year. Look at **verse 7**. These consecrated animals were being sacrificed to "*goat demons* with which they play the harlot." The Hebrew word used here is *sâ'îr*. What were these "goat demons"? Well, we see this word in other places in Scripture. In Isaiah 13:21 and Isaiah 34:14, we see these "goat demons" live in open fields, ruins, and desolate places. It makes sense that Leviticus 17 teaches that Israelites were offering sacrifices to these goat demons in "open fields." In 2 Chronicles 11:15, we read that Jeroboam even had high places constructed for these goat demons. Simply, goat demons were what Israelites believed lived in *ruin cities* that they came across. Ancient inhabitants of these places would worship these goat demons because they thought that these goat demons would increase their harvest. Do you see what was going on with the Israelites? They would **sacrifice to God** at the Tabernacle and also **sacrifice to goat demons** in the open fields. They were mixing pagan practices with what God told them to do. God essentially tells them that they are committing adultery with Him.

How often do we get on to the Israelites for doing things like this? How often do we say, "Are you serious? God has made Himself evident among you. He has done miracle after miracle. He freed you from Egypt in incredible ways. He sustained you in the wilderness. He led you with fire and a cloud. Why in the world you worship goat demons?" Yet, how many times do we come to church with our "offerings" to God and then turn around and absolutely *worship* things of the world? Satan is not creative. He is not creating new strategies. Just like he convinced the Israelites to worship goat demons *in addition to* worshipping God, he deceives us by thinking we are being a "good Christian" when we come to church even though our lives can be devoted to so many worldly things. Listen, there are *goat demons* all around us. There are things absolutely crying out for our attention. During the average day, how much time to you give the Lord versus how much time do you give worldly things that have no eternal significance? See, we can jump on the Israelites for worshipping goat demons, but don't miss the fact that we often do the same thing.

God says in verse 7 that it will be a **permanent statute** throughout the generations. **This week, don't offer sacrifices to goat demons. Don't commit adultery with your God by sacrificing your time, money, or energy to things** of the enemy. **Instead, devote yourself to the one, true, living God. He is all you need. Don't let Satan deceive you into thinking that his way is better. It's not!**

Let's keep going in our text. **Read Leviticus 17:10-14.** Now we get to some teaching on the *blood* of the animal. God did not want the people eating blood. What happens if they ate blood? What did it say in verse 10? God would *set His face against them* (that just sounds scary, right?) and they would be *cut off* from the people. This is serious business. Why was it so serious? What did God say is in the blood? **Life**. And that life is given to make **atonement**. Slow down with me right here for just a minute. Think about this. It's is big when understanding the gospel story. Way back in Leviticus 17, God says that **life** is in the **blood** and also **atonement** is in the **blood**. When a sacrifice is made, what did they do with the blood? They put it on the altar. Why? **Shedding of *innocent* blood made atonement for *sin*.** It was a substitute. Innocent blood was given in place of sinners. In this case, God accepts the blood of the animal, which is the life of the animal, in place of human blood and human life. Therefore, Leviticus 17 teaches that **any** blood belongs to God! It is the **life** of that living animal. So, Israelites were to *never* eat the blood.

Did you know that this was counter-cultural at the time? There was an ancient practice of *eating* and *drinking* blood. Why would anybody want to drink blood? Any ideas? There was this thought that if you ingested blood, you would have special divine powers. You are drinking the **life** of the animal. There were people drinking animal blood as a superstitious practice, thinking they would be like God. God says, if you consume the blood, you are going to feel my wrath. You are not to attempt to be *Me*.

That sounds logical, right. Today, if you are a Jew who absolutely *loves* God's Word and wants to obey it, would you be drinking blood for any reason? No. Jesus comes along. What does He teach? *Unless you **eat** my flesh and **drink** my blood, you don't have life.* That is John 6. Do you see the tension here? Do you see why it might be hard for some Jews to follow Jesus? Yes, it is a new covenant. We understand that. But if you have grown up believing that the Torah should be the central aspect of your life, and in it, it says not to drink blood, it makes it difficult to follow. Right? Now, Jesus' intent was to give a display that **He abides in each believer**. We understand that. But feel the tension a Jew has with that symbolism.

As we finish today, I want us to think about how this chapter relates to us as believers. We read in the New Testament about arguments on what laws Gentiles needed to follow when they became believers. Acts 15 tells of the council of Jerusalem's decision: Gentiles must stay away from things sacrificed to idols, **blood**, **things strangled**, and fornication. *Two* of the four laws they decided on were pulled straight from Leviticus 17. Now, why would they want to pull out these laws on blood for Christians? They understood that Christians needed to have the proper view of blood if they were going to understand the importance of Jesus' blood being shed for them on the cross!

The Passion of the Christ is a movie that really packs a punch for Christians. There is one scene in the movie that absolutely stands out...the scourging scene. It must be absolutely impossible to be a believer and *not* have a reaction when those Roman soldiers deliver blow after blow to Jesus' body.

Watching this scene always reminds me of Jesus' words to His disciples during the Last Supper.

> *"And when He had taken a cup and given thanks, He gave it to them, saying, "Drink from it, all of you; for this is **My blood** of the covenant, which is **poured out** for many for forgiveness of sins." Matthew 26:27-28*

The blood of Jesus was literally **poured out** to cover our sins! No, it was not just a few ounces. He was beaten so profoundly that He was *disfigured to the point of **not even looking like a man*** (Isaiah 52:14). In the process, His blood left His body so that it might cover the sins of all His followers.

> *"And according to the Law, one may almost say, **all** things are **cleansed with blood**, and **without shedding of blood** there is **no forgiveness**." Hebrews: 9:22*

I am so thankful for His blood. I hope you are, too. Our *atonement* is **only** because of His blood. Leviticus 17 is clear, *"the life of the flesh is in the **blood**."* Our salvation is *not* from anything else.

> *"For you know that it was **not** with perishable things such as silver or gold that you were redeemed from the empty way of life handed down to you from your ancestors, but with the **precious blood of Christ**, a lamb without blemish or defect." 1 Peter 1:18 (NIV)*

We stand **redeemed** because of the **precious blood of Christ**. Why, then, would we live our lives devoted to *perishable things*? Why would we live our lives exalting *money* or any earthly thing? That is not what has redeemed us! That is not where our salvation lies. **Our lives are to glorify the One who gave every ounce of His blood to cover our sins!** Does that describe your life right now?

Actively Guarding His Instructions

In chapter 17, we talked about how there would be a shift in theme for the rest of the book. What did we say would be the focus? **Holiness**. Leviticus 18 begins to offer some specific laws about Israel's behavior. The next two weeks (Leviticus 19 and 20) are closely related to today's lesson. As a matter of fact, Leviticus 18-20 is considered a unit. Now, I want you to look at your Bible. There is a repeated phrase in these three chapters. What is it? *I am the Lord (your God)*. It occurs almost **fifty** times in these three chapters! As God is giving the Israelites all of these instructions about His preferences, He constantly reminds them that He is *their* God. He has *chosen* them. He *loves* them. And He has the *authority* to make the rules because He is God.

Read Leviticus 18:1-5. God did not want Israel to engage in pagan practices. Don't do what the Egyptians do. Don't do what the Canaanites do. Instead, do what I tell you!

Now, *if* Israel was going to be a holy nation, God knew that He would need to begin by setting specific boundaries for the family. Do you remember what God had promised Abraham? He promised Abraham that he would be the ancestor of a great nation. For a great nation to exist, there must be strong family units. God begins to make some very specific instructions about families in Leviticus 18.

Leviticus 18:6-18. These verses deal with incest. For Israel, God truly needed specific laws about incest. Why? First of all, we previously discussed that God did *not* want Israel intermarrying with pagans. ESPECIALLY the Canaanites. We looked at Deuteronomy 7:3-4 as we discussed this point.

> *"Furthermore, you shall not intermarry with them; you shall not give your daughters to their sons, nor shall you take their daughters for your sons. For they will turn your sons away from following Me to serve other gods; then the anger of the LORD will be kindled against you and He will quickly destroy you."*

There is a problem! If Israel had to marry one of their own, they would be tempted to marry people close to them. Like *very* close to them. Maybe even people that grew up in the same house that they did. God needed to make sure that they knew He wanted them to marry other Israelites, but not actually their brothers and sisters.

There is another reason that God needed to clarify the importance of marrying someone outside the immediate family. Today, if you go to Israel, you still see ancient walls that define family *nahalas*. When Israel reached the Promised Land, each family was given a *nahala*. In the Bible, it is referred to as the family's inheritance. Their family land was their most prized possession. They protected it at all cost and wanted to make sure it stayed in their family. So, marriages often were between relatives to keep the family *nahala* intact.

I tell you these things so that you can see why these laws in Leviticus 18 are so important. In verse 6, it says that a person is not to approach any "close relative" or "blood relative" to "uncover nakedness." The NIV says to "have sexual relations." Just so you know, "uncover nakedness" is a Hebrew idiom that really does to have sexual relations.

What constituted a "close relative"? The Hebrew word (*sheer*) is specifically a nuclear family member of a mother, father, son, daughter, brother, or sister. That is defined in Leviticus 21:2. In our verses, there are twelve unacceptable relationships mentioned. We will not look at this in great detail, but it is also something that is worth studying.

Read Leviticus 18:19-23. There are five issues addressed in these verses.

1. *No sexual relations during menstruation (v. 19)* – We discussed this when we discussed the uncleanness of a woman during her menstruation explained in Leviticus 15.

2. *No adultery (v. 20)* – Adultery is prohibited in other places as well (Exodus 20:14, Deuteronomy 5:8, and John 8:2-5). What was the punishment for adultery? Both parties were to be put to death (Lev. 20:10; Deut. 22:22). Even among other people groups in the ancient Near East, we see in other sources that adultery was called "the great sin." If you don't understand the seriousness in which God views adultery, then you will never understand the severity of metaphor when God says that we commit **adultery** when we worship other gods instead of Him! We are to be loyal to our husband!

3. *No offspring offered to Molech (v. 21)* – Who was Molech? He was the god of the Ammonites (1 Kings 11:7) and he had the head of an ox. When a couple had their first child, they were required to put that child onto the burning arms of the iron structure of Molech. Why would they do that? They believed it would ensure financial prosperity for the family and for future children. This became very real to me when I was in Tel Arad two years ago in Israel. We stood next to a location that was pre-Israelite in which little babies were sacrificed more than likely to *this* god. When Israel came into the Promised Land, He says, "Don't do that. Don't sacrifice your kids to foreign gods."

4. *Homosexually prohibited (v. 22)* – How does God describe the offense? An *abomination*. We see this word used many times in the Book of Deuteronomy. In those cases, it is used for *idolatry* and *inappropriate worship of God*. In Mesopotamia, there was a saying. "If a man has anal sex with a man of equal status – that man will be foremost among his brothers and colleagues." However, God makes His preferences clear to Israel. *Don't practice homosexuality. It is an abomination.* By the way, if any of you want some New Testament references, you may want to jot

down Rom. 1:27, 1 Cor. 6:9-11, 1 Tim. 1:10, and Rev. 22:15. Do you know what the Biblical penalty was for homosexuality? Death (Lev. 20:13).

5. *Bestiality prohibited (v. 23)* – Bestiality was actually more common than you might expect at this time. We know from Hittite law that if a person had any sexual relations with cattle, sheep, or pigs, they received the death penalty. However, if a person had sexual relations with a horse or a mule, there was no penalty. Egyptian records show that some of their cults practiced bestiality. In our class, we talked about some of the things that happened at Caesarea Philippi. People practicing bestiality in order to entice the god Pan to come out from the underworld and give fertility. So, God had to tell Israel – *Don't get caught up in that stuff.* The penalty for this was also death (Ex. 22:19, Lev. 20:15-16, Deut. 27:21).

Read Leviticus 18:24-25. The end of Leviticus 18 paints a picture. Do you remember us talking about the people defiling the Tabernacle earlier in Leviticus? We said that there had to be offerings given for the Tabernacle because of sin. Leviticus 18 essentially says that the entire Promised Land is to be *holy.* The previous inhabitants of the land were "vomited out." How is that for a mental picture? However, God warns His people. *If you do these things listed in Leviticus 18 like the pagan nations before you, you will also be* **vomited out** *of the land (v. 28).* Just think about the word God uses – vomit. It is the most *violent* of all bodily reactions we have. It is a picture of God's absolute repulsion when He sees the activities of Leviticus 18 being performed. It makes Him want to vomit! Do you think He is serious about believers understanding His heart on the matters of Leviticus 18? Absolutely!

As we finish looking at this chapter, I want us to go back to the beginning and revisit where we started.

> *You shall not do what is done in the land of Egypt where you lived, nor are you to do what is done in the land of Canaan where I am bringing you; you shall not walk in their statutes. You are to perform My judgments and keep My statutes, to live in accord with them; I am the LORD your God. So you shall keep My statutes and My judgments, by which a man may live if he does them; I am the LORD.*
> **Leviticus 18:3-5**

It was a Friday night. We would be boarding an airplane the next morning to come back to the United States. The leader of our mission trip asked us to write down the *highs* and *lows* of our time in Portugal. I searched around for paper and found a napkin. When I found it, I started jotting down notes. The overwhelming *low* that week was simple...**seeing so many people who were *lost* and had no idea.** You see, 81% of the people in Portugal claimed to be Roman Catholic, but less than 3% actually attended mass. Overall, only 3% of the population claimed to be evangelical Christians. *My heart broke looking at these people who **claimed** the tradition of being a "Christian" but were absolutely and utterly **lost in their sin**.*

The napkin still reminds me today of a time when God took me on a trip to teach me about Himself.

In Leviticus 18, God was taking His people on a trip...though theirs would be permanent. He took them from the land of Egypt into the land of Canaan. But He specifically warned them **not** to do what they witnessed in these lands. In Egypt, there was much idol worship. On top of that, there was a law passed saying a man could marry his own sister. God tells His people to **stay away** from these things even though it was the *norm* for the Egyptians. In Canaan, *magicians* and *star worship* were common. In addition, there was much incest.

Leviticus 18 explains, in very specific detail, that He did not want His people to be defiled by engaging in the sexual immorality they were being delivered *from* in Egypt or *into* in Canaan. Instead, He instructed them to **keep** His statutes and His judgments. The word used here for **keep** (*shāmar*) means *to guard pro-actively; quick to employ offensive as well as defensive measures to protect.* God did not want His people to be persuaded to live like the earthly society they were placed around! He had a higher calling for them! So, He tells them to **actively protect** that which He instructed them to do.

Why was it so important for them to **actively keep** His instructions? It was the *only* way they would **live**. The Hebrew word used for **live** (*ayah*) conveys the act of *the Lord infusing His amazing life in believers through faith.* If His people wanted the God of the Universe to impart **His life** *into* them, they had to *pro-actively* keep His commands.

God is essentially telling His people in Leviticus the same message we read in Romans:

> *"And **do not be conformed to this world**, but be **transformed** by the renewing of your mind, so that you may prove what the will of God is, that which is good and acceptable and perfect." Romans 12:2*

Thinking back to my week in Portugal, I left a country that has overwhelmingly *conformed* to this world to go to another country that has overwhelmingly *conformed* to this world. In both the United States *and* Portugal, statistics would have you believe that *most* people believe in Jesus. The problem is that there is no **transformation**. People just don't look like Him! Without **transformation**, *there is no infusion of His amazing life!*

*Will I **actively** protect the Lord's instructions? Listen, you may not have an ongoing temptation to bestiality. That is not the culture around us like it was at the time of Leviticus 18. But there are many other worldly temptations around us. Will we actively protect what God says, rather than what the world says? If I am going to do that, my life must be **set apart** and **different** than the world around me. The driving force in my life must be allowing Jesus to **live through me**. I must not be satisfied* *with living a comfortable "Christian" life that looks like the broken world in which I have been placed.*

Like God repeats almost 50 times in Leviticus 18-20, **He is the Lord our God**! Let's live our lives for Him.

The Progression of Forgiveness

Today, we will be looking at **Leviticus 19**. Jews teach that *this* chapter more so than any other in the entire Bible explains what it meant for Israel to be a holy nation. We could spend the next three months in this chapter, examining so many things. Worship to fairness in commerce. Legal proceedings to reverence for the Temple. Idolatry to avoidance of pagan practices in family relations. Using God's name to support the needy. Giving first fruits to theft and fraud. Honestly, this chapter has it all.

A couple of things that I found interesting when doing some research about Leviticus 19. Did you know that Leviticus 19 is essentially a repeat of the Ten Commandments? Look at the following table:

	Exodus 20	Leviticus 19
I am the Lord	v. 2	vv. 3, 4, 9, 12, 14, 16, 18, 25, 28, 30, 31, 32, 33, 35, 37
Graven images	vv. 4-6	v. 4
God's name in vain	v. 7	v. 12
Sabbath	vv. 8-12	vv. 3, 30
Honor parents	v. 12	v. 3
Murder	v. 13	v. 16
Adultery	v. 14	v. 29
Stealing	v. 15	vv. 11, 13, 35-36
False witness	v. 16	vv. 16, 11
Coveting	v. 17	v. 18

Another thing I found interesting is that the book of James uses Leviticus 19 as its basis. While we aren't going to focus on this today, it is very intriguing to consider.

For this chapter, I just want us to just look at a couple of different things based out of Leviticus 19.

Read Leviticus 19:9-10. This is talking about Pentecost (or Shavuot). The text says that the people were not to reap all the way to the edges of their fields. Why? They are to be left for the **poor** and the **stranger**. God wants *us* to care for the *poor* and the *stranger*. We see this principle all over the Bible. It is **not** a handout! The poor and the stranger had to work. They had to come and glean the portion of the field for themselves. Can you think of a Biblical story when you see this practice lived out? **Ruth 2 – Boaz and Ruth.**

Do you have any idea how much they were to leave in their corners? God doesn't say. Rabbis began to teach that the *minimum* that a person had to leave in their corners was 1/60th of their field. Many left **more** than that. *Why?* We said that this happens at Shavuot (or Pentecost). What does Shavuot celebrate? It is a celebration of **thanksgiving**. Once a year, your *nahala* would show everyone else how thankful you were to God. If you left big corners, you are showing that you were extremely thankful for all that God had provided. If you left 1/60th of your field, it filled the law, but it also said that you weren't really all that thankful.

Right now, if someone looked at your *nahala*, would they see that you have **big** corners reserved for the poor and strangers? Or would you need a microscope to find the tiny corners that you are leaving for others?

Read Leviticus 19:17-18.

> *You shall not hate your fellow countryman in your heart; you may surely reprove your neighbor, but shall not incur sin because of him. You shall not take vengeance, nor bear any grudge against the sons of your people, but you shall love your neighbor as yourself; I am the LORD.*
> **Leviticus 19:17-18**

I *love* the Church. I *love* my church family in Hohenwald. I *love* the sweet conversations I have had with believers all over the world. I *love* the instant connection I feel with them even when I don't speak their language. I *love* being in the family of God.

*Unfortunately, we live in a fallen world. Even though my love overflows as I think about the Church, there have been countless times someone in the Church has let me down for one reason or another. So, what do we do when this happens? Leviticus 19 gives us a **progression of forgiveness** that I think can help us learn what to do when another believer hurts us.*

I want to point a couple of things about the text out before we look at that progression of forgiveness. First of all, notice that there are several subjects in our text: *fellow countryman, neighbor, sons of your people.* These verses were specifically talking about fellow Israelites who were missing the mark for some reason. They were fellow believers. As we think about how to apply this forgiveness in our lives, we are specifically talking about what to do when it is a fellow Christian. Secondly, you might read verse 17 and say, "Now I don't **hate** anybody, especially not another believer in Jesus." The word that is translated as hate (*śānē'*) doesn't really mean to *hate bitterly*. If you look at this word used all throughout the Old Testament, it really means *to love less* or *to regard indifferently*. THIS IS A HUGE DIFFERENCE! If someone in this church body has done something to you and you don't have the same **love** for them as you do other believers, then you *śānē'* them. If someone here has wronged you and you look at them with indifference rather than love, you *śānē'* them. God has made His preferred will crystal clear in this: He wants us to be **unified** in the body of Christ and to **love** one another. Be honest in your heart right now. Who do you *śānē'*? Who are the believers that you try to avoid talking to? Who are the believers that you honestly wish would just find another church? Who are the ones that you don't **love** the way you should? Are you with me? Are your toes stepped on? You need to see their faces. Then, we can look at what God tells us to do about it.

Let's just imagine we are an Israelite in the audience and God has given us these instructions. A fellow Israelite just did something to us. What did the text say we should do about it?

1. **<u>Reprove</u> (*yākaḥ*) them** - This word means to *argue on the basis of sound, legal reasoning; to offer reproof needed to properly settle a dispute.* If a fellow Israelite wronged you, the first step would be to offer **sound reasoning** that would stand up in a court of law. This is where the record needs to be set straight. Too many times, things can get swept under the rug just because we don't want to have a difficult conversation. Let's look at a couple of other verses where this word is used. **Read Proverbs 3:12** - *For whom the LORD loves He **reproves**, even as a father corrects the son in whom he delights.* God **reproves** those who are off-base. And He often uses *us* to be His mouthpiece for the reproving when a fellow believer needs correction. **Read Proverbs 28:23** - *He who **rebukes** a man will afterward find more favor than he who flatters with the tongue.* When is the last time you **rebuked** someone other than one of your children? *As a Christian, God calls us to **reprove** other Christians who are missing the mark by offering sound Biblical reasoning. This is the first step.*

2. **Avoid taking <u>vengeance</u> (*nāqam*)** - This word means to *avenge* or *vindicate.* If a fellow Israelite wronged you, God forbid you to take matters into your own hands! **He** is the judge, not you! He says so in Deuteronomy 32:35 and Psalm 94:1. In both verses, He says that **vengeance** is His! *As a Christian, if another Christian wrongs us, we may **reprove** them, but not **take vengeance** upon them. That is God's job, not ours!*

3. **Avoid bearing a <u>grudge</u> (*natar*)** - If a fellow Israelite wronged you, you were not to stop at *avoiding vengeance* with that person. You were to **not even hold a grudge** against that person. Have you ever been so mad at someone that you had anger stored up and you were ready for the perfect opportunity to let that person know how you felt? That is exactly what this word means. God says, "Don't ever have anger stored up in your heart against another believer." *As a Christian, the next step of forgiveness is to **not even think** about the times we have been hurt. How hard is it to truly forgive **in the same way** Christ forgave us (**<u>Ephesians 4:32</u>** - Be kind to one another, tender-hearted, **forgiving** each other, **just as God in Christ also has forgiven you.** <u>Colossians 3:13</u> - Bear with each other and **forgive** one another if any of you has a grievance against someone. **Forgive as the Lord forgave you.**)? This is our call as believers! Not to bear a grudge. Instead, forgive like Christ forgave us. Completely! Guess what, the progression of forgiveness doesn't even stop there!*

4. **Love that person as yourself** - If a fellow Israelite wronged you, you were not to stop at *avoiding vengeance* with that person. You were not to stop at *forgiving* them and *not holding a grudge* against them. God ups the ante. He says to **love** that person that wronged you. Later, there were two men that cited this verse as a summary of how we are to treat others. **Jesus** (Matthew 22:39-40) and **Paul** (Romans 13:9). *As a Christian, the ultimate display of forgiveness is **love**. How hard is it to love someone when they have wronged you? **Very**. Which is why it is hard to imagine what Jesus did for us on the cross! That was **grace**. And that is what we are to give others, just as Jesus gave it to us!*

As we finish discussing this chapter, consider a couple of things. God wants you to leave big corners on your field for those less fortunate than you. And for those that don't know Him. How generous are you to those God has put around you? It is not just money. It is time. It is energy. It is listening to problems. It is encouraging them. Do you have big corners? Maybe today you know that you have corners so small that nobody else can even see that they are there. God wants to use *you* to show others about His goodness. We must leave large corners in our fields.

Lastly, is there someone in your church that you *śānē'*? Is there someone who has hurt you and you are still holding onto it? Today is the day that the progression of forgiveness needs to be set in motion. They may have no idea that they have even hurt you. Oh, how our Heavenly Father wants us to be a unified body so that He may use us to the max. I beg you. Search your heart. It is time to forgive. It is time to love. It is time to be a living example to the world of what Jesus does for us.

My Golf Clubs

Leviticus 20 is very similar to Leviticus 18. Many of the same things we have already discussed are also present in this chapter. Let's begin by reading **Leviticus 20:1-5**. We talked about the worship of Molech in Leviticus 18. It was a disgusting practice of child sacrifice. One interesting thing is how God uses a play on words that you will miss if you don't look at the original Hebrew language. Three times it talks about a person "giving" their child to Molech. God says that He will "set" His face against that person. It is the same word. God says, "If you *give* your child to Molech, then I will *give* my personal attention to punish you for that." It is a picture that you will miss if you aren't digging into God's Word. His Word is so rich. Don't be satisfied with a surface reading. He will show you incredible truths if you are hungry!

Much of chapter 20 deals with improper sexual relations, just like Leviticus 18. The difference between the two chapters is the **intended audience**. Leviticus 18 addresses the would-be offender of the law. Its attended audience is the one who is doing the sinful act. Leviticus 20 addresses the Israelite community. The offender must be punished by others in the community.

As with our discussion in Leviticus 18, what do you see is the common punishment for the offenses listed in Leviticus 20? Seven times, it says that the person who violated the law "shall surely be put to death" (vv. 2, 9, 10, 12, 14, 15, 16). God is telling the Israelites – you better get this right! There is something that I want you to think about. What types of crimes did God demand the strongest punishment for? What type of crimes did He give the death penalty? It was crimes against **Him** or against **family**. That is so counter-cultural. In the ancient Near East, do you have any idea what laws were in place at the time that demanded the death penalty? It was almost always violations that resulted in **economic loss**. Don't miss this. God's laws placed more value on **life** than on **material or possessions**. The culture placed more value on **material or possessions** than on **life**. Does that ring a bell?

Read Leviticus 20:22-24. Much of this is just a review of the things we have already discussed. We are to **keep** God's instructions. Who can tell me what that means? It is to *pro-actively guard with offensive and defensive measures.* We are to **not follow** the customs of the world. Then, it talks about Israel possessing the Promised Land. How does God describe it? "A land flowing with milk and honey."

Milk and honey – what do you see if you picture this? Rich, fertile land that has everything you need. In the Middle East, that is **not** the image. *Milk* is the product of the shepherd. They produce milk by their flocks. They didn't have cows, so milk came from goats. *Honey* was the product of a farmer. But it is not what you think it is. There are two types of honey in Israel – bee honey (what we are used to) and fig/date/fruit tree honey (more like jam to us). Both types of honey have the same Hebrew word – *devash.* The honey of the Bible is almost assuredly the jam honey. How do we know? In **Deuteronomy 8:7-9**, God describes the seven types of food He would give His people in the Promised Land. Wheat, barley, vines (grapes), figs, pomegranates, olive oil, and honey. All of these foods are plant-based except for honey (if he is talking about honey from bees). Jewish literature is very clear. They say that the honey in this list is the jam made from fruit (they say it is from dates). *Honey* is a product of the farmer.

Another Biblical place that we see the context of **milk and honey** is found in Isaiah 7. Isaiah says that the King of Assyria will turn the land into a land of milk (not of milk and honey). That meant that he would kill the farms so much so that the only thing you could do is pasture flocks. He says that every place that there used to be a thousand vines will become briars and thorns. And in those very spots will be oxen and sheep. That is a big curse. He says that the *shepherds* will take over and the *farmer* will be driven out. It will no longer be a land of milk and honey.

I just want you to understand that milk and honey was not really a promise of the richness of land like we think. It was a picture of a place where the shepherd and the farmer could both live. And that was unusual in that part of the world. Most countries were either the land of the shepherd or the land of farmers, not *both*.

It is a powerful image. Why? God says that He is both our **shepherd** and our **farmer**:

> **Psalm 23:1** – "The LORD is my **shepherd**, I shall not want."
> **Isaiah 5:7** – "For the **vineyard** of the LORD of hosts is the house of Israel And the men of Judah His delightful plant."
> **John 10:14** – "I am the good **shepherd**, and I know My own and My own know Me,"
> **John 15:1-2** – "I am the true **vine**, and My Father is the **vinedresser**. Every branch in Me that does not bear fruit, He takes away; and every *branch* that bears fruit, He prunes it so that it may bear more fruit."

Yes, God was leading His people into a land of the *shepherd* and the *farmer*, but they were not to forget who their true shepherd and their true farmer was. They were to depend on *Him*. When we began the discussion on honey, we talked about Deuteronomy 8:7-10. Now listen to some of the next verses.

> *When you have eaten and are satisfied, you shall bless the LORD your God for the good land which He has given you. Beware that you do not forget the LORD your God by not keeping His commandments and His ordinances and His statutes which I am commanding you today; But you shall remember the LORD your God, for it is He who is giving you power to make wealth, that He may confirm His covenant which He swore to your fathers, as it is this day (Dt. 8:10-11, 18).*

Let's unpack one other verse in Leviticus 20 today.

Thus you are to be holy to Me, for I the LORD am holy; and I have set you apart from the peoples to be Mine.
Leviticus 20:26

This may seem a little odd if you are not a golfer, but my golf clubs are special to me. You see, I *know* each of them very well. My putter has been with me for 22 years now. That Ping Zing 2 has made many putts for me. The same can be said of my sand wedge. For 22 years, I have learned how to use my Ping Eye 2 wedge to hit a multitude of shots around the green. My driver has been in my bag for several years. I know that the ball will fly

low off the Nike clubface with a little draw. My irons are incredible. Each of my Titleist irons gives me confidence when addressing the ball because they have always been so reliable.

I love **my** golf clubs. Why? Because they are *mine*. Each was chosen after careful consideration because they were just right for *me*. But understand something else. Every one of my golf clubs is in my bag to achieve a common goal...to get the little white ball in the small round hole with as few shots as possible. While they share a common goal, each club has a distinct purpose. If I am 100 yards from the green, I am not reaching for my 4-iron. If I have a 25-foot putt, I am not grabbing my driver. **My golf clubs share a common goal yet have different strengths in reaching that goal.**

There is an age-old question: *What is the purpose of life?* Allow me to let God's Word answer this question.

> *"Everyone who is called by My name, And whom **I have created for My glory**, Whom I have formed, even whom I have made."*
> *Isaiah 43:7*

The purpose of my life is to glorify my Heavenly Father! Our text today in Leviticus 20 teaches His will is for us to be **holy "to Him."** We are to be *set apart*. We are to be *different*. We are to be *like Him*. Why? The text specifically says our holiness is **"to Him."** Our holiness is *not* for **us**. Our holiness is for **God**. The text continues by saying that we have been set apart **"to be Mine."** The purpose of our life is to point people to Him! *Why do I, so often, make it about **me**?*

In the very same way that each of my golf clubs have an overall purpose of executing the will of their owner, each follower of Jesus Christ the exact **same** overall purpose! Each of my golf clubs have different strengths but *all* have the same overall purpose. That sounds a lot like Romans 12.

> *"For just as we have **many members** in **one body** and all the members do **not** have the **same function**, so we, who are many, are one body in Christ, and individually members one of another. Since we have **gifts that differ** according to the grace given to us, each of us is to **exercise them accordingly**: if prophecy, according to the proportion of his faith; if service, in his serving; or he who teaches, in his teaching; or he who exhorts, in his exhortation; he who gives, with liberality; he who leads, with diligence; he who shows mercy, with cheerfulness."* Romans 12:4-8

God *chose* me. He *knows* me. He wants me to use the *strengths He has placed within me* to glorify Him!

In Scripture, there are 19 different spiritual gifts discussed. It is absolutely crucial that each believer *knows* the spiritual gift(s) that God has entrusted. Each one of us is different. God has gifted each of us uniquely to meet the purpose for which He created us. Do you know your gift(s)?

Now, if that spiritual gift is the golf club that God has given you, it has a very specific purpose. When I was younger, I had to go to the driving range a lot to find out *exactly* how far I could hit each club. I would want to know how far I could hit the ball if it was in the back of my stance and I was hitting it low. I would want to know how far I could hit the ball if it was forward in my stance and I was hitting it high. How far would it go if I cut across it and made it slice? It took a lot of practice. But the practice pays off. Your spiritual gift has to be developed through practice. Are you actively practicing your gifts?

A couple of words of caution. First of all, don't guess about your gift! This is one of the things we must take very seriously. We can't get this wrong. If God wants you to *use* your gifts, I better know *exactly* what they are and not guess at it. Another word of caution – we can be tempted to say, "Well, that is not my gift" when something comes up that we don't want to do. Over and over in Scripture, God uses the **weakness** of people to show the world His **strength**. One of my friends is an incredible man of the Lord, but his gift is *not* speaking. What if he stood before our congregation next Sunday morning and delivered a Spirit-filled sermon like has never been preached from the pulpit? Who would the congregation **know** that it would have come from? The Lord! **2 Corinthians 12:9** talks about God's power being perfected in our weakness. We must listen to the Lord moment by moment for His instructions. There are times that He will tell us that something is not our job because we are not gifted in that area. But there are times when He wants to show the world His mighty strength by putting us in positions that do not fit our strength so others will know that it is coming from Him!

- Just because our gift may not be **giving**, doesn't mean that we are never to *give*.

- Just because our gift may not be **mercy**, doesn't mean that we are never to *have mercy*.
- Just because our gift may not be **helps**, doesn't mean that we are never to *help*. I can identify with this! Serving is not something that comes naturally to me like it does my wife. Does that mean I should never serve? Does that mean I should just say, "Julie, it is your job to do all the serving because God has gifted me in different ways"? Absolutely not! I am to earn from her because that is her gift and she can teach me what it looks like to serve.
- Just because our gift may not be **evangelist**, doesn't mean that we are never to *evangelize*.
- Just because our gift may not be **teaching**, doesn't mean that we are never to *teach*.

Know your gifts but know that there are times when God may put you in a position in which you aren't as strong to display His strength to the world!

As we finish today, I just want you to think one last time about my golf clubs. They don't get to tell their master *where* or *when* they may be used. I use them as I see fit. I know which club to use in each situation. As His child, we are **His**. He gets to use us *where* and *when H*e wants! He knows exactly how to use us in every situation.

*Will we live a life that is truly **His**?*

The Good Samaritan

We will look at **Leviticus 21** today. Let's start by reading **verses 1-3** and **verses 10-11**. There is a New Testament story this is very familiar to you in which these laws are seen in action. Does anyone know the story? Turn to **Luke 10**. We are going to spend the rest of our time looking at this story.

Read Luke 10:25. The lawyer is an expert in Jewish law. Understand that he was someone who debated and trusted his own knowledge in this story. He thought he could put Jesus on trial. That was his motive. He thought he could see if he was really Messiah.

"Teacher, what must I do to inherit eternal life?" There is something wrong with the question before we even get to the answer. There is *nothing* we can do to earn salvation. It is by grace through faith. Every other religion has a method by which you can earn God's favor so that when you die, you go to your grave *hoping* that you have done enough for salvation. We don't do that as Christians. We live everyday knowing that Christ *was* good enough. We trust in acts of righteousness, just not our own. We trust that Jesus earned God's favor. As long as He is accepted, we are accepted through Christ by faith.

Jesus answered the question in a different way. Look at **verse 26**. He answers a question with a question. *"What is written in the Law?"* This is how a Jewish rabbi would answer a question. They answer questions with questions. The lawyer knows the Torah. He quotes **Leviticus** and **Deuteronomy**. Look at **verses 27-28**. What if your salvation depended on loving God with everything you have all the time? It is impossible. We can't do what the Law requires. We must trust the one who did it for us.

Do you see what just happened? This man asked Jesus what he had to do to be saved and the response was: You must do something you *can't*. This lawyer knew that. He knew he was a sinner. He knew that he had no hope of loving God with everything he had all the time. He could not do it. And neither can we. Even our good deeds are like filthy rags.

There was a moment right here in the story where this man had a chance to confess his need of a Savior. Is that what he does? No. He goes in a different direction. Look at **verse 29**. He wanted to *justify himself*. This is the problem with all of us. In our brokenness, we have a need to justify ourselves. Why do you think there are so many other man-made religions? Their basis is to justify ourselves by our works. The gospel says that we can never be good enough, yet there was a man who died for us while we were still sinners. It is good news for the sinner. Christ came, lived a life we could never live, took our place in judgment, and says, "My yoke is easy, rest in Me."

This lawyer could not swallow his pride and accept a Savior. He had status. Others in the community looked at him as righteous. He couldn't humble himself enough to admit that he wasn't righteous. So, he asks Jesus a question – *"Who is my neighbor?"* Before we look at how Jesus answers this, I want you to think about something. Does the answer even matter? Part of the answer is to love *"your neighbor as yourself."* Let's just say your neighbor is the person you love more than anyone else in the world, do you *really* love them just as much as you do yourself? If we are being honest, we are absolutely *selfish* in our flesh. Am I wrong? Tell me you think about your spouse and his or her interests more than you think about yourself. Do you see the problem here? Even if the neighbor was the person we love most in this world, we are in trouble if our eternal salvation is based on our love for them.

Honestly, I am already guilty of this standard. I don't always love God with all my heart, soul, mind, and strength. And even if my neighbor is my wife, there are times when I love *myself*, *my thoughts*, and *my ways* more than her. I am guilty!

Let's just continue by looking at Jesus' response to the man's question – *"Who is my neighbor?"* By the way, you can read Jewish literature and find that this was a **huge** question at the time period. There was a lot of debate. Basically, it was universal that *one* people group were **not** considered neighbors. Want to guess what people group that was? We will see that group in our story. It is the Samaritans.

You need to understand something else about the culture. There were two groups of people that looked at the Bible very differently at the time of Jesus. One group took the Torah literally. They did not put any stock in oral tradition or any other book after Deuteronomy. But they were *very* literal when it came to the text. The other group used the entire Old Testament as well as oral traditions that had been passed on since the time of Moses. Do you know the name of the two groups? **Sadducees** (took it literally) and **Pharisees** (used entire Bible and oral traditions).

What do I mean when I say "oral traditions"? Well, the Pharisees believed that God gave the Torah, but He also based other teachings that were not written down. They believed you needed to obey the Law of the Torah, but they also believed that there was an overarching principle to God's instructions. That principle was *pikuach nefesh*. This means *human life is the most important thing*. So, if there is someone who falls into a pit on the Sabbath, you violate the Law of Sabbath and do work to get them out, because *life* is more important than *laws*. Someone who submitted to oral tradition would say, "Yes, God doesn't want a priest to touch a dead body, but if a life is in danger then that law goes out the window because, to God, life is the most important thing." That is *pikuach nefesh*.

Who is my neighbor? Jesus answers this question by telling a parable.

Read verse 30. Jerusalem to Jericho is a 17-mile stretch known in their time as the *Path of Blood*. I want you to see a **picture** of this road.

It is a foot and a half wide with a cliff on one side. As we read that people in this story *pass by on the other side*, know that Jesus is illustrating a point. Picture them trying to scoot around this man on an 18-inch road. They were *forced* to deal with this man. On this path were robbers. People were commonly mugged and killed on this road. What happens to the man in verse 30 makes sense. After beating this man and stripping him, the robbers left him **half dead**. This was a Hebrew concept from the word *goses*. It means someone between life and death. Picture this man. Bloody. Beaten. Left on the road. He has no hope. Now, if someone just followed the Torah, what would he do with this person? Walk right past. If someone also adhered to the oral tradition, what would he do? Even if he was the High Priest on Yom Kippur. He would stop and help him because of *pikuach nefesh*.

In **verse 31**, a priest walks by. There is *hope*. This priest is this man's hope. But he **passed by** the man. What is going on here? Is this just a terrible priest? No. He is a **Sadducee**. He wants to obey the Torah. He is coming from a seven-day consecration ceremony in Jerusalem and traveling to Jericho to perform his priestly duties. What happens if he touches this man? Leviticus 21 is clear – he becomes *defiled* (verse 1). He becomes unclean for seven days (Numbers 31:19). And even if he *did* touch this man, the man was half dead. He may not have even survived. For all we know, this priest's heart broke for this man, but he could not have performed his priestly duties in Jericho if he stopped to help him. The thing I want you to understand is that he was **obeying Torah** by walking past this man.

In **verse 32**, we see a Levite walk by. Another hope! Did he stop? Nope. He passed by as well. It's easy to get on to these guys, but understand the Torah tells them *not* to touch this man. This Levite was also a **Sadducee**. He is doing *exactly* what the Law told him to do.

Now, the original audience would absolutely expect the next person to be walking by to be a **Pharisee**. Would they have expected him to help this man? Absolutely! They believed in *pikuach nefesh*. But that is not what happens. Look at **verse 33**. (Stop after Samaritan). A Samaritan? Really? A little background. In 722 BC, Assyria was the world power. They starved towns. They murdered and robbed everyone they conquered. They came through and conquered the northern kingdom of Israel. The southern kingdom (Judah) watched as Assyria brought people into Israel and intermarried with the people left in Israel. These Israelites began worshiping the pagan gods as well. How do you think the Jews in the south felt about this? They said, "You are worse than pagans. You are half-breeds. And you are worse than dogs." Several other things happened that we don't have time to get into with the Samaritans leading up to the time of Jesus. Just know that there was a **ton** of tension between the Jews and the Samaritans at the time of Jesus. It was so bad that we see the exchange between Jesus and the woman at the well in John 4 where she stops Him after one sentence and says, "Wait a minute. You are a Jew. I am a Samaritan. We don't speak." Jews and Samaritans absolutely *hate* each other. They are enemies.

The priest and the Levite do not help this half-dead man. But, here comes a **Samaritan**. Read the rest of **verse 33**. What did this man have? Compassion. What did he do? He bound up this man's wounds. Do you think he had a first aid kit? No. He probably tore his own garments to bandage up those wounds. He poured oil and wine to cleanse the wounds. He puts this man on his animal. So, what is the Samaritan doing? He is walking. Probably partly naked because he has used his own clothes to bandage this man's wounds. He is walking in this condition down the *Path of Blood*...risking his own life for this stranger that he didn't even know. The text says he takes him to an inn and takes care of him. Scholars say that the closest inn at that time would have been at least 12 miles away!

Look at **verse 35**. This is crazy. *On the next day....* Have you ever had your schedule inconvenienced for a stranger that took you into the next day? I mean, we may have a conversation that takes 15 or 20 minutes, but the next day? And he takes out money. This half-dead man is not only costing this Samaritan time but now it's costing him money. And then he says that he will pay whatever else is needed when he comes back. He gives the innkeeper a **blank check** for his enemy. What is wrong with him?

Jesus asks, *"Which of these three was the neighbor?"* In verse 37, we see this lawyer is never going to say the word Samaritan, but his response is, *"The one who showed him mercy."* Jesus says, *"You go and do likewise."*

Here is the thing about this parable. We read it and think, "Am I more like the priest, the Levite, or the Samaritan." That is *not* the point. The point of the parable is not for us to stop and help someone that is hurting! That is not even close to the point! Who is our neighbor according to this parable? The Samaritan! Our neighbor is our *enemy*. Jesus is telling us to love the ones we hate the most.

That is the secret of the Kingdom of Heaven. Who is it that turns your stomach? That person is in God's image, too. Even a Samaritan is a neighbor.

There is one other thing about this story. You see, the Samaritan points us to another man. A man who binds wounds. A man who will go without so others will go with. A man who is moved by compassion. A man who risked his own life to save another. Jesus is the ultimate Good Samaritan.

So, who are *we* in the story? If Jesus is the Good Samaritan, who are we? What condition was the man on the road? He was half dead. Jesus saw us for what we really are. Dead. He *did not* pass us by. He wasn't too busy for us. He had **compassion** on us and *couldn't* pass us by.

Imagine with me what happened on the day the half-dead man woke up. He is wrapped in another man's clothes. His wounds are bandaged. He has had oil and wine in his wounds. He must have woken up confused. I mean, the last thing he remembered was probably being jumped on the road. Now, he has been cared for and he is in a place that he doesn't recognize. Imagine as he asks the innkeeper what happened. I am guessing the exchange went something like this:

> **Innkeeper**: "You will never believe this. Your enemy stopped for you."
> **Man**: *"What do you mean, I was dead?"*
> **Innkeeper**: "You were dead, but now you are alive because this man stopped for you."
> **Man**: *"Where is he?"*
> **Innkeeper**: "He has gone away."
> **Man**: *"Will I ever see him again?"*
> **Innkeeper**: "I bet you will. He said that he would come back."

Put yourself in that man's shoes. You are in an inn in Jericho and you are thinking, "How in the world am I going to thank the man who saved my life?" Listen to the words of Jesus – **Go and do likewise**.

How do we respond to the gospel? We give our lives for the sake of others. That will never happen if we aren't asking God to break our hearts with His compassion. Let's go and do likewise by loving even those that are our enemies! Parables have a point. They are to show us how to live out God's Word. Do you **love** your neighbor? Really? Do you love even those people that have wronged you? Be like the Good Samaritan this week and love on *everyone*, including those who don't like you.

The Perfect Offering

Turn **Leviticus 22**. Do you remember what scholars call Leviticus 17-26? The Holiness Code. As we continue to look at God's instructions on holiness, today we are looking at two different areas: The *priest's* holiness and the *offering's* holiness. But I want to begin by looking at how important it was for Israel to get this right. Read **verses 1-2**. What would happen if the priests were not careful with offerings made to the Lord? What does He say? It would **profane His holy name**. We *must* understand this concept! This is a big deal.

I want to give you a little review. We talked about this way back in Leviticus 5. We have two options in everything we do: (1) We can **hallow the name** (*Kiddush HaShem*) or (2) we can **profane the name** (*Hillul HaShem*). **Kiddush HaShem** means that we live in such a way as to bring glory to God among those who do not know Him. The idea is to associate loving deeds with the reputation of God. When we previously discussed this concept, we talked about a story of a Jewish rabbi who lived 100 years before Jesus. He was poor and his disciples bought him a camel from a wealthy Arab trader. As this rabbi combed through the mane, a jewel fell out. The disciples rejoiced. Their rabbi was now rich! Only the rabbi said, "No, this doesn't belong to me." He took it back to the Arab trader. The Arab looked at him and said, "Blessed be the God of Simeon ben Shetach." This is what it looks like to **hallow** the name.

So how do you **profane** the name? How do you *Hillul HaShem*? Anything that makes others think *less* about our God is profaning His name. We can *profane* God's name by not representing Him well as His priests. We can *profane* His name by not being honest with those around us. We can *profane* His name by point people *away* from Christ rather than *towards* Christ. With all of that in mind, think about the Lord's prayer with me. The Lord's prayer begins by saying, "Our Father who is in Heaven, **hallowed** be Your name." Our role as believers is to continuously live lives that *hallow* the name of Jesus. We are to make much of Him and always bring glory to Him.

Leviticus 22 begins by saying, *if you get the things I am telling you wrong, you are* **profaning** *My Name. Hillul HaShem.* He wanted Israel to be incredibly careful in treating *holy* things in a *holy* way. What are some *holy* things that we don't always treat as *holy*? Turn to **Exodus 31:12-17**. The Sabbath is supposed to be our wedding band to the world. The Sabbath isn't just a Jewish thing. Read Hebrews 4! God *expects* us to have a wedding band to show the world that we belong to Him. That wedding band is treating the Sabbath has *holy*. It is treating the Sabbath as our date night with our husband. When you treat it as just a normal day, you **profane** it. And you **profane** Him. *Hillul HaShem.*

The Priest's Holiness:

Read **verse 3**. Even priests weren't perfect. Throughout the course of the day, there were times that they became unclean for various reasons. God wanted to make sure that they **never** contacted anything holy while they were unclean. Holy things should never be defiled. What was the penalty if they touched something that was holy when they were unclean? They would be *cut off*. Never again would they be able to serve at the altar as a priest. They were finished.

The next few verses talk about things that make a priest unclean. We have discussed these previously, so we aren't going to look at them today.

Look at **verses 10-11**. The question is *who* can eat the priest's portion of the holy offerings. We see something surprising in these verses, at least to me. Slaves purchased by the priest and children born to them after they have come into the priest's household may eat the holy offerings. Bonus points will be given to you if you can tell me another time in the Old Testament that slaves are given a special benefit because of the lineage of their master? **Genesis 17:12-13**. Abraham was told to circumcise slaves and they became *covenant* people because of their master.

The first half of Leviticus 22 focuses on making sure the priest is holy so that he may handle the sacrifice. Before we move to the next section, I just want you to think about this question: *As God's priest (1 Peter 2:5-9), can you say that you are different from the world? Can you say that you are **holy**? Old Testament priests could never handle anything that was holy if they were defiled. Is there something that you need to repent of today? Is there something that is making your heart beat out of your chest right now because you know it's not what the Lord wants?* **Be holy as He is holy.** Be set apart. Be a royal priesthood that is busy doing the will of the Master. And if anything in your life isn't lining up to that job description, get it straight today!

The Offering's Holiness:

Read **verses 20-23**. Not only did the *priest* have to be holy, but the offering had to be holy as well. It had to be **perfect**.

> **Whatever has a defect, you shall not offer, for it will not be accepted for you. When a man offers a sacrifice of peace offerings to the LORD to fulfill a special vow or for a freewill offering, of the herd or of the flock, it must be perfect to be accepted; there shall be no defect in it.**
> **Leviticus 22:20-21**

Have you ever *expected* one thing but *received* something entirely different? In high school, I was asked to design a t-shirt for our tennis team my senior year. I created an image and gave it to our coach. I *expected* that image to be a small pocket-sized logo on the shirt. The day the shirts arrived, my jaw dropped as the logo was a massive image across the front of the shirt. It looked *terrible*!

What does God expect out of offerings? God instructs the offerings given to be **perfect**. If the offerings were not *perfect*, what does He say about them? He says they would not be **accepted**. The Hebrew word used means *acceptable because meeting necessary standards*. **Perfection** was the standard for offerings. They couldn't be blind. They couldn't be lame. They couldn't be sick. Can you think of a time in Scripture when people were offering animals that were blind, lame, and sick? **Malachi 1: 7-9, 13-14.**

We read stories like this and think, "*How could you offer God something that is defiled when He has been so clear in His instructions that He wants a perfect offering?*" But I wonder how often I give Him *offerings* that He looks at and says, "You can just keep that for yourself, Mark." How often are my offerings *substandard*? How often do they *not* meet His expectations?

The human tendency is to *keep the* **best** for ourselves and give God *leftovers*. Listen, He made it clear years ago: **He expects our absolute best if we want Him to** *accept* **our offering!** As a matter of fact, He wants our offering to be *perfect.* This seems like a tall order. How are we going to give Him a *perfect* offering? After all, anything our flesh touches becomes *tainted.* So how will our offering ever be **perfect**? How will we ever give Him an *acceptable* offering?

> "*Therefore I urge you, brethren, by the mercies of God, to* **present your bodies a living and holy sacrifice,** <u>**acceptable**</u> **to God,** *which is your spiritual service of worship.*" *Romans 12:1*

A **perfect** and **acceptable** offering to Him is when we give Him 100% of ourselves! If we are giving Him 99% of our life and holding on to the final 1%, He looks at us and says, "No, thank you." The call of a follower of Christ is to live a **crucified life** by dying to our flesh and allowing **Christ** to live *through us* (Galatians 2:20). **Don't miss this: The only way we give God a** <u>**perfect**</u> **offering is if Jesus Christ is the One making that offering within us.** Understand that you cannot *die to yourself* and hang on to **anything**!

Have I really **died** *to my flesh? Does He have* **all** *of me? If not, I am giving Him an offering that is* **unacceptable***.*

Because those t-shirts I designed in high school were not what I expected, they really were not acceptable. You know, I never actually wore that shirt. If God does not have **all** *of me, how will I ever expect Him to use me in a mighty way for His kingdom?*

As we finish, I want us to end our lesson in the same way we started. Read **verses 31-33.**

> *So you shall keep My commandments, and do them; I am the Lord. You shall not profane My holy name (**Hillul HaShem**), but I will be sanctified (**Kidush**) among the sons of Israel; I am the Lord who sanctifies (**Kidush**) you, who brought you out from the land of Egypt, to be your God; I am the Lord.*

When we obey the Lord, we **increase** His reputation among the nations. People think more of Him if we walk the walk. When we don't obey Him, we **decrease** His reputation. We profane His name (Hillul HaShem). This may surprise you, but I have always been a *Whitehead*. Growing up in a small town like McKenzie, everyone knew my parents. My dad was a dentist in town. My mom had grown up in the town and knew everyone. When I went to school, I followed in the footsteps of my brother who is 4 years older than I am. Does anybody else have an older sibling that you were compared with throughout school? I feel your pain. There was a **standard** that had to be met in being a *Whitehead*. I always felt like I couldn't let down my parents. I never wanted to do anything that would bring shame to my family.

How much more important is it that we bear the name **Christian** well? Like it or not, you represent Jesus. You can't duck out of that responsibility. People judge Him based on how you act and what you say. You bear His name. Right now, can you say that you are **increasing** His reputation and **decreasing** His reputation by your words and actions?

Jesus in the Holidays

The LORD spoke again to Moses, saying, "Speak to the sons of Israel and say to them, 'The LORD'S appointed times which you shall proclaim as holy convocations—My appointed times are these:
Leviticus 23:1-2

We see God's appointed holidays listed in Leviticus 23. We will go through each of them and think about their purpose and how they point to Jesus. But first, why do you think God made specific holidays for His people? *Each holiday is a reminder of some great thing God has done for His people.* Before we start looking at each festival, I want to remind you of something. Jesus, the disciples, and the early church all celebrated these festivals. Another thing that we need to keep in mind is that each Jewish holiday is a prophecy that looks forward to what God will do in human history. So, these festivals that we are going to look at in Leviticus 23 are a part of God's master plan. I think it is important for us to understand each of them.

THE SABBATH (verse 3)

The first holiday mentioned in Leviticus 23 is the Sabbath. Many Jews would say that God lists this holiday first because it is the most important of all of them. Think about it. It is observed every week while all of the other holidays are only once each year. What does the word "sabbath" mean? *Rest.* Every seventh day (beginning on Friday night at sunset and continuing until Saturday night at sunset), God told His people to *rest.* Does anybody know why Jews make a point to say that it should start at sunset, rather than sunrise? *Genesis – "There was evening, and there was morning, the first day."* All of God's days, from the time of creation, begin at *sunset.* God created the world in six days, then He *rested.* He gave us a model.

There is something else to understand. The Sabbath reminds a Jew of *salvation.* Do you realize that the Jewish people did not observe the Sabbath until *after* they were delivered out of Egypt? So, the Sabbath reminds a Jew that there is a day coming when a Messiah will *save* them. It is a day of *salvation.*

Isn't it interesting that Jesus came and called Himself the "Lord of the Sabbath"? Isn't it interesting that He makes a promise to give *rest*? "Come to Me, all who are weary and heavy-laden, and I will give you rest. Take My yoke upon you, and learn from Me, for I am gentle and humble in heart; and you shall find **rest** for your souls" (Matthew 11:28-29).

I think we have this view that the Sabbath to a Jew is a day of legalism. It is a day when they must count their steps from the edge of the city and not go too far. It is a day that they can't pick up objects. On my recent trip to Israel, we arrived on Friday evening. By the time we made it to the hotel, it was after sunset. I have a question for you. How do you get your luggage to your room when it is the

Sabbath in Israel? If you are a Jew, you can't hike it up the steps. That's work. But you also can't push the button in the elevator. That is also work. So, they have a system. When the sun goes down on the Sabbath, the elevators open on every floor. You never have to do work by pushing a button.

I use that illustration because we think it is silly. Listen, they are doing their very best to obey the Lord. Do you realize the *longest* commandment of the Ten Commandments is God's instructions about the Sabbath? The Jews are doing their best to obey Him. And, let me tell you, the Sabbath is not some monotonous ritual. It is a day of *joy*. It is a day of giving the Lord a fresh commitment of following Him.

In the 4th century before Christ, a ritual began at the end of the Sabbath. It was a home celebration "for the benefit of the children." It was called *Havdalah*. As the sun went down on Saturday evening, families would get together and usher out Sabbath with *Havdalah*. It was a time when parents wanted to pass on their beliefs to their children and answer any questions they may have. Turn to **Acts 20:7-12**. Notice Paul was talking on the "first day of the week" *until midnight*. Again, the first day of the week begins Saturday night when the sun goes down. Scholars believe that Paul was ushering out Sabbath with *Havdalah*. And this is the setting of this young man falling asleep and falling three stories. *Question for you that have kids in here. What if we had Havdalah in our families? What if we set aside a time each week to explain to our children our beliefs and answer questions that they may have?*

One final thought about Sabbath before we move on to the next portion of Leviticus 23. Last time we met together, we talked about Sabbath. Do you remember what God calls the Sabbath in Exodus 31? He calls it a **sign** of their relationship with Him. It is the wedding band to the world that they were married to Him. So, do you think the Sabbath is important to God? Do you think it matters to Him that His people have a day set aside for resting in Him?

PASSOVER: THE FIRST OF THE SEVEN ANNUAL HOLIDAYS (verses 4-5)

The first of the seven annual holidays is Passover, which begins God's yearly calendar. "This month shall be the beginning of months for you; it is to be the first month of the year to you" (Exodus 12:2). Passover takes place during the spring, when the earth is full of new life, after the cold "death-like" state of winter. It makes sense that God's calendar would start in the Spring. It certainly makes more sense than beginning the new year in the dead of winter, as we do in the Western world.

Just as Passover begins God's calendar, it also marks the beginning of Israel's history as a free nation. We all know the story of the Passover and how God saved His people in Egypt by having them put blood from a lamb around their door.

Before the Temple was destroyed in Jerusalem, *most* Jews would travel to Jerusalem to celebrate Passover. Each family would bring a spotless lamb to sacrifice. The lambs reminded Israel of the lamb sacrificed in Egypt on the night they were delivered. The lamb also reminded them of the blood price that was needed for their sins.

Did Jesus celebrate Passover when He was here on earth? Yes! In Luke 2:41-42, we see Jesus and his family travel to Jerusalem for the Passover feast when He was 12 years old. Right before He is crucified, He is in Jerusalem for Passover. He has the Passover Seder. He dies at exactly 3:00 – the time for the Passover sacrifice. 1 Corinthians 5:7 says that Christ *is* our Passover. And, just like the Passover lamb (Ex. 12:46; Num. 9:12), none of His bones were broken (John 19:33, 36).

Passover was also a prophecy of a greater redemption, a more profound Exodus, and a more excellent Lamb which was to come. John the Baptist understood this when he said, "Behold the Lamb of God, who takes away the sin of the world." Passover was a prediction that God would one day send His Son into the world to be the ultimate sacrifice, to shed His blood on a cross, so that God may "pass over" the sins of those who believe in the Messiah. As a result, He will bring us out of our Egypt, our bondage to the world, our slavery to sin, our captivity to the flesh and our slavery to the enemy. The Lord will take us by the hand, lead us through the wilderness of this world, to the New Jerusalem. It's no coincidence that Jesus died on Passover. His last supper was a Passover Seder and He died the next day, the first day of Passover – in fulfillment of Passover. We will see a similar pattern throughout the rest of the holidays. Each one looks forward to something that the Messiah would accomplish. It is amazing how God used the holidays in the life of Jesus.

FEAST OF UNLEAVENED BREAD (verses 6-8)

The Feast of **Matzah** (Unleavened Bread) begins with Passover and continues for seven days. Nothing with yeast is to be eaten during that period. Why do you think they were to eat matzah during this feast? One reason why Jews eat matzah is to remind themselves of their hasty departure from Egypt. By eating matzah, Israel remembered that, when God did redeem them, He redeemed them quickly...so quickly that there wasn't even time for their bread to rise.

There is, however, another reason why Israel was to eat matzah. Throughout the Scriptures, leaven is often used as a symbol of sin. Just as a little bit of leaven will quickly spread and infect an entire batch of dough, so a little sin will quickly spread and infect an individual or an entire community. Prior to Passover, Jewish families will spend days, and even weeks, systematically ridding their homes of leaven. Paul was familiar with this ceremony of cleansing homes of leaven. He wrote to the Community of messianic believers at Corinth: "Your boasting is not good. Don't you know that a little leaven leavens the whole lump of dough? Clean out the old leaven, that you may be a new lump, just as you are unleavened, for Messiah our Passover Lamb has been sacrificed. Therefore, let us celebrate the

Feast, not with the old leaven, the leaven of malice and wickedness, but with the matzah of sincerity and truth" (1 Corinthians 5:6-8). Paul used the ceremony of cleansing the house of leaven to teach us to cleanse our lives of sin if we expect to enjoy the blessings of Jesus, our Passover Lamb.

At His Last Supper (which we already said was a Passover Seder), Jesus took the unleavened bread, broke it, and gave it to His disciples, and He gave this matzah new meaning when He said, "This is My body which is given for you. Do this in remembrance of Me." In essence, Jesus was declaring, "I am the fulfillment of this unleavened bread; I am the first man who has lived in this world and who never sinned." He did resist every temptation, and finally, on the Feast of Matzah, Jesus' sinless life was put to death on the cross, destroying the power of sin. The Bread of Life (John 6) died as our Matzah. And He was buried on the Feast of Unleavened Bread. During this day, there is a prayer that Jews pray – "*Give us life out of the Earth.*" I don't think that is a coincidence.

THE FEAST OF FIRST FRUITS (verses 9-14)

The Feast of First Fruits is the third yearly holiday, and also takes place during the week of Passover. Passover begins on the evening of the fourteenth of Nisan. First Fruits takes place on the sixteenth day of Nisan, which is the third day of Passover. This was a feast that thanks God for His gift of the harvest. It also was to thank God for bringing Israel into the Promised Land after their captivity in Egypt.

In ancient times, when the Temple still stood in Jerusalem, on this day Israel's High Priest took the first sheaves of the barley harvest and waved the first fruits of barley as a wave offering. This ceremony was like a prayer; by waving the first fruits of the harvest, the High Priest was, in essence, praying: "Lord God of Israel, thank You for the beginning of this year's harvest. We offer to You the first fruits of this year's harvest. Lord, accept the first fruits, the beginning and the best of the harvest. O Lord, accept us, Your people, and please bring in the rest of the harvest." If God would accept the offering of the first fruits, it was a guarantee that He would bless Israel with the remainder of the harvest during the year.

What did this look like for the common Israelite? There was a problem. God did not really tell Israel exactly *how much* of their harvest that Israel should offer. Rabbis got together and decided that a common Israelite should offer 1/60th of their harvest. They also decided the only acceptable harvest to offer are *wheat, barley, grapes, figs, pomegranates, olive oil, and dates (or devash)*. These are the same things God promised to give Israel when they entered the Promised Land in Deuteronomy 8. Their offering told God, "We trust You to provide the rest of the harvest."

How does this feast relate to Jesus? The Feast of First Fruits was a prophecy that the Messiah, who died on Passover, would come back to life. Death would not be able to hold the Sinless One. God would raise Him from the dead. He would be offered up as the "first fruits of those who have fallen asleep" (see 1 Corinthians

15:20). That means that Jesus is the beginning of God's harvest of humanity, the first to be raised from the dead. As the first fruits, He is the beginning and the best, the prototype and model for all those joined to Him. Because God found Him acceptable, raising Him from the dead as the first fruits, it is a guarantee that those who believe in Him, the rest of the harvest of humanity, will likewise be raised and be given eternal life.

Don't miss this. Jesus was raised from the dead on the Feast of First Fruits. It was "on the third day" that Jesus rose from the dead. Passover starts the evening of the fourteenth day of Nisan. First Fruits take place on the sixteenth day of Nisan. So, you have part of the fourteenth day, the whole of the fifteenth day, and the third day, the sixteenth day of Nisan, on which falls First Fruits. Listen - the very same day the High Priest was offering the first fruits of the barley harvest, God was raising the Messiah from the dead as the first fruits of redeemed humanity. The Feast of First Fruits is the true Biblical Resurrection day.

What if Christians embraced this God-given holiday with its symbolism of the resurrection, rather than replacing it with Easter eggs, bunnies, and ham?

SHAVUOT (verses 15-22)

Let's review the first three spring feasts: *Passover, Feast of Unleavened Bread (Matzah), Feast of First Fruits.* We know the importance of **Passover**. It is a holiday that reminds us of what God did as He saved His people by delivering them out of Egypt and into the Promised Land. A price had to be paid for that freedom – a spotless lamb that was sacrificed and its blood used over the doorframe. The **Feast of Unleavened Bread** is a seven-day feast in which Jews have always searched their house for days, even weeks beforehand looking to get rid of yeast. Think about it. Leaving Egypt was a quick process. The hard part was for God to get Egypt out of them! So, the Feast of Unleavened Bread takes longer than Passover. It is a time of removing leaven...removing sin...removing Egypt so that they could be completely devoted to the Lord. The **Feast of First Fruits** celebrates the beginning of the barley harvest. It is when the people wave their first fruits to God to say, "Thank you." It was also a time of thanking Him for the harvest that was to come. This was on the "day after the sabbath" (Lev. 23:11). So, what day would first fruits fall on? *Sunday.* Again, Jesus rose from the dead on the Feast of First Fruits as the "first fruits of those who have fallen asleep" (1 Corinthians 15:20).

The next holiday on God's calendar is **Shavuot** which means "weeks." Why would it be called "weeks"? Read **Leviticus 23:15-16**. This holiday was supposed to be *seven weeks and one day* after the Feast of First fruits. So, in Hebrew, it is called "weeks" or *Shavuot.* Why do we call it Pentecost? Pentecost is the Greek name for this holiday. It means "fiftieth" because this holiday takes place on the fiftieth day after First Fruits. In Acts 2, we see Greek-speaking Jews. They call the holiday *Pentecost*, but understand it is the exact same holiday as *Shavuot*, just in the Greek language rather than the Hebrew language. Pentecost did **not** start in Acts 2! It is a holiday that had been celebrated since the Torah was given.

Let's talk about the Jewish history of the holiday. Why did they celebrate Shavuot?

1. It was a *thanksgiving* for the early *barley* harvest and first fruits of the *wheat* harvest. Get this straight in your minds. **First Fruits** was a celebration of the first fruits of **barley** and **Shavuot** was a celebration of the first fruits of **wheat**. It is the beginning of the wheat harvest.

    We read a few minutes ago about Shavuot. The people were to make two loaves of bread and wave them before the Lord. Was it to be *with* or *without* leaven? In contrast to Passover, this bread was actually supposed to contain leaven. We have said before that leaven represents sin in the Bible. Why on earth would God want this offering to contain leaven? The short answer is that the people *were* sinners. The only offering they could really give God would be imperfect. However, God loved them with their imperfections. It reminds me of Romans 5:8 – *"While we were yet sinners, Christ died for us."* The love of God is not dependent on our perfection.

    Because their offering was imperfect, what else did God require them to offer on Shavuot? Seven male lambs, one bull, and two rams for a *burnt offering*. One male goat for a *sin offering*. And two male lambs for a *peace offering*. Pop quiz – What is the other name for a *peace offering* that we talked about way back in Leviticus 3? *Fellowship offering*. **Every single Pentecost**, these animals were offered to the Lord as a way of saying, "We know we are not perfect, and, even our token of thanks is flawed." We will come back to this thought in a minute.

2. It was the anniversary of receiving the Law at Mt. Sinai. Did you know that? When the people were celebrating Shavuot (or Pentecost) at the time of Jesus, there was a great celebration of Moses getting the Torah (including the Ten Words [Commandments]) at Mt. Sinai. We read in Exodus 19:1 that the children of Israel reached Mt. Sinai "in the third month." Without getting too complicated, if you do the math of the number of days listed at the beginning of Exodus 19 from when the children of Israel reached Mt. Sinai until when God shows up and gives the Torah, it puts you right at Shavuot. From the literature that was found with the Dead Sea Scrolls (written about 250 years before Christ), we know that Jews at the time of Jesus absolutely celebrated Shavuot, not only as a thanksgiving for the harvest, but as a thanksgiving for God revealing His Word to them!

What did Shavuot look like at the time of Jesus? Remember that this was one of the three pilgrim festivals. What were the other two? *Passover and Sukkot.* Every Jew is going to be in Jerusalem at this holiday. Picture 2-3 million people in a city of 60,000. And you thought Oktoberfest was bad! This is the setting of Pentecost.

Celebration in the Temple: People flooded the Temple on the morning of Shavuot. They came with their two loaves of bread made with the finest flour as commanded by God. They also brought the *seven spices* that we have mentioned previously that we see in Deuteronomy 8:8. Mid-morning (around 9:00) would be the time to sacrifice all the offerings we mentioned a few minutes ago. The lambs, the bull, the rams, and the goat were offered. While the offerings were taken place, there were **three specific readings** that the priest would read on the platform in the Temple:

- **Exodus 19 and 20** – The story of God showing up at Mt. Sinai and giving Moses the Torah. When God shows up, the people heard the *sound of wind, fire* comes down, and God speaks as *thunder (kolot).*
- **Ezekiel 1 and 2** – This is Ezekiel's vision where God appears with *fire* and Ezekiel heard the *sound of wind.*
- **Ruth** – The entire book of Ruth was read because it takes place during this time of year and it also emphasizes Leviticus 23:22. God's presence is shown by how His people care for the poor. We are going to look at this in more detail in a moment.

Every year around 9:00, the people are reading about these things in Exodus and Ezekiel. Fast forward to **Acts 2**. What happened?

> *"When the day of Pentecost came, they were all together in one place. Suddenly a* **sound like a mighty rushing wind** *came from heaven and filled the whole house where they were sitting. They saw tongues like* **flames of fire** *that separated and came to rest on each of them. And they were all filled with the Holy Spirit and began to speak in other* **tongues** *(kolot) as the Spirit enabled them." Acts 2:1-4*

Sound of wind and fire appeared. All of a sudden, there is *kolot*. It is just what they had been reading! God is reenacting His story that happened 1300 years earlier at Mt. Sinai and 600 years earlier in Ezekiel's vision! Don't miss that.

Now, when all of this happened, where were the disciples? We think Pentecost happened in the Upper Room. There isn't even a hint of that in Scripture! Luke (24:53) says the disciples *were continually at the Temple praising God*. This is how the book of Luke ends. Pentecost is a feast at 9:00 in the morning at the Temple. Where would good Jews be? At the Temple! Where would the disciples be if they were *continually* in the Temple praising God? At the Temple! Also, where would there be thousands of people to be saved? Certainly not in some Upper Room. They would be at the Temple. Then, 3000 people were baptized. Where can you find enough baptistries to baptize 3000 people? Well, at the Southern Stairs of the Temple, there have been over 100 *mikvoth* (plural for *mikveh*) found. People had to *mikveh* before going into the Temple to worship. So, there was enough *mikvoth* to baptize all that came to Christ that day. Listen, they are at the Temple! The text says that the sound *filled the House*. That is the Temple. That is what the Jews call it! It is referred to as "The House."

Do you understand what happen in Acts 2? God wasn't satisfied with the House He was living in. At 9:00 in the morning at the time of sacrifice, God showed up. There is *wind*. And God shows up in a ball of *fire* that separated and rested on each of them. The magnificent Temple was not where He wanted to live. Sure, it was absolutely beautiful. But He wanted to live in us. How did He get to us? Do you remember what is just in front of the Holy of Holies in the Temple? There is a veil. What happened as Jesus died? It tore. From top to bottom! We think that it tore so that we would have access to Him. While that is true, I think there is more to it. It tore so He could get out. And He came out and found a *better* house. To Him, a more beautiful place. A place that His presence could be portable. On Pentecost, God changed His address!

In the Bible, we see that God has had 3 houses. First, the tabernacle. Then, the Temple. Finally, *us*. People don't have to go to a Temple to find forgiveness of sins anymore. They can encounter Him when they meet *us*. That is why He wanted a portable house. You are God's Temple because God's Spirit lives in you. God wants Heaven and Earth to meet wherever you go. He wants people to come in contact with God Himself when they meet you.

When God showed up at the Tabernacle, fire showed up and the people responded by shouting for joy and falling on their faces (Leviticus 9:23-24). When God showed up at the Temple, fire showed up, people responded by bowing down and shouting, "God is good, and His love endures forever" (2 Chronicles 5:1-14; 7:1-3) Question - What happens when others meet Him in us? Do they know the goodness of God and His amazing love because we are displaying Him to them?

Understand another important point about being us being the Temple. You (plural) are the Temple (singular) of the Holy Spirit. It is made up of a bunch of stones. We are living stones being shaped into His House. That is what Scripture says in 1 Peter 2:5. God has one body made up of a bunch of stones. Together, *we* are the Temple. We are not individual Temples! When you get to a day when you don't feel God's presence, seek out someone in the community! We are *one* body and we need each other. We cannot forsake meeting together as His body.

So, what is Pentecost? On the very same day 1300 years earlier that God's people were given the Law, 3000 died. What happens 1300 years later? The Holy Spirit shows up and 3000 believed. It is a real-life picture of **2 Corinthians 3:6** – *"The letter kills, but the Spirit gives life."*

Going back to the instructions of Pentecost in Leviticus 23, God's Word says that the people were not to cut the corners of their fields. Why? He wanted them to **care for the poor**. As a matter of fact, during Pentecost, the custom was for Jews to invite the poor to celebrate with them. This is why the book of Ruth has always been read on Pentecost. So, if it is a real Pentecost, the poor will be cared for as we keep the corners of our field uncut. What happened at the end of Acts 2?

> *"They devoted themselves to the apostles' teaching and the fellowship, to the breaking of bread and the prayers ... all who believed were together and had all things in common. 45 And they were **selling their possessions and belongings and distributing the proceeds to all, as any had need**. 46 And day by day, attending the Temple together ... they received their food with glad and generous hearts, 47 praising God and having favor with all the people. And the Lord added to their number day by day those who were being saved."* – Acts 2:42-47

In the OT, the poor were fed at the Temple. Why? God wanted to know that He cares for the poor. If you are the Temple, God will send the poor to you.

During Pentecost, God changed His address from a Temple to *us*. Do you understand how God sees you? He would rather live in you that some incredible Temple in Jerusalem! He thinks you are absolutely beautiful. And He wants those who come in contact with you to meet Him. If they do, they will respond with shouts of joy and worship. We need to be unified as His Temple. And we must care for the poor as His representatives.

Pentecost is here. We are the *third* Temple. Let's be the Temple He wants us to be by putting Him on display to our world and allowing Him to live through us. Allow others to encounter Him as they meet us.

THE FEAST OF TRUMPETS (verses 23-25)

We have talked about all four of the Spring feasts: *Passover, Feast of Unleavened Bread (Matzah), Feast of First Fruits*, and *Shavuot*. What type of harvest First Fruits celebrated? *Barley*. What about Shavuot? *Wheat*.

Spiritually, just as the four spring holidays are connected, so are the final three Fall holidays. They are connected to Jesus' Second Coming. They all take place in the seventh month – the month of completion. If the pattern evidenced in the Spring holidays holds true for the Fall holidays, they too will be fulfilled on their own day. The Fall holidays will bring to completion God's plan to rescue humanity. The first Fall holiday is the Feast of Trumpets. It takes place on the first day of the seventh month, which is the month of Tishri. Among the Jewish people, it is more commonly referred to as "**Rosh HaShana**" – the Jewish "New Year." It may be the traditional Jewish New Year, but it is not the Biblical New Year since this holiday begins the seventh month. According to the Bible, the true "Jewish New Year" takes place during the spring at Passover time. The Lord clearly stated this to Moses in Exodus 12:2 when He said, "This month shall be the beginning of months for you; it is to be the first month of the year to you."

On the first day of the seventh month, God told His people to rest and blow the shofar, a special trumpet made from a ram's horn. The shofar was blown in ancient Israel for various reasons:

- If there was danger, the shofar was blown.
- If important information was being proclaimed, the shofar was blown.
- If people were gathering for an appointed time or a special event, the shofar was blown.
- If the people were preparing for battle, the shofar was blown.
- If the king was coming to visit a town, the shofar was blown.
- If a new king was being crowned or a new high priest was being appointed, the shofar was blown.
- If a bridegroom arrives to claim his bride, the shofar was blown.

When Jesus returns at the 2nd coming, do you understand that He will be fulfilling *every* Biblical indication of the blowing of the shofar? The shofar on the Feast of Trumpets (or Rosh HaShana) is saying that our King and High Priest is here! He has arrived and is ready for battle. And He has come as our Bridegroom, ready to claim His bride.

Read **1 Corinthians 15:51-52**. In a moment, the shofar will be blown. Our Bridegroom will be here to get us, and we will be changed. It is an allusion to the Feast of Trumpets. Knowing this, the text continues by saying, "Death is swallowed up in victory. O death, where is your victory? O death, where is your sting? This Feast is a yearly reminder that there is a day coming that the Messiah (Jesus) is coming back. He IS the victor. Death is not the end. Read **1 Corinthians 15:58**. If we *know* that Jesus is coming back and we will join Him on the winning team, the text says that we should **always** be *abounding in the work of the Lord*. **Always**. As in, there shouldn't be a moment that we are working for *ourselves* rather than *Him*. Why? When we work for Him, it will never be in vain. This Feast of Trumpets reminds us that there *will* be a day when we will be **recompensed** for all of the time, money, energy we spent "abounding in the work of the Lord." When we listen to His voice and do what He tells us to do, it is *never* in vain. Ever. There will be a reward one day. So, stay faithful. Keep listening for that shofar to sound. It is coming!

Read **1 Thessalonians 4:13-18**. Verse 16 teaches that there will be a shofar blown on the day the Lord returns to get us. Why? That is the signal of a king. That is the signal of a high priest. That is the signal of a bridegroom. That is the signal that a war is about to take place.

In **Matthew 24:31**, we see Jesus talking about His return. What does He say will accompany that return? A great trumpet. A great shofar.

In the book of Revelation (**11:15-17**), Jesus returns to Earth at the sounding of the seventh trumpet (or shofar). The shofar is designed to wake up the bride. It is designed to get the bride ready for the 2nd coming of Jesus! That is what this feast is about. It is about waking up the bride and getting her ready for what is in store.

THE DAY OF ATONEMENT (verses 26-32)

Ten days later, Yom Kippur, the Day of Atonement, takes place. We actually discussed this day when we were in Leviticus 16. If you remember, we said that this was the **most important** day for a Jew. This was the one day when the High Priest could enter into the Most Holy Place in the Temple, sprinkle blood on the ark of the covenant, and atone for the sins of Israel. I would encourage you to go back and listen to Leviticus 16 this week on YouTube, if you get a chance. If you remember, we talked about the two goats...one of them named *azalel*. We aren't going to go into a lot of the specifics of that today since we already covered it.

Let's talk about how it is celebrated. Yom Kippur is a very solemn day. Unlike the other holidays we have been discussing, this is a *fast* rather than a *feast*. The Jews fast, pray, and ask for forgiveness on Yom Kippur. The rabbis teach that Jews have ten days from the beginning of the Feast of Trumpets to the close of Yom Kippur in which to repent. These ten days are called "The Days of Awe." These days are intense. They are filled with prayer and self-reflection. It is a time when relationships are to be restored, forgiveness is to be offered, and reconciliation is to be sought. Why is it so intense? According to this tradition, if you do not repent during those ten days, God will blot your name out of the Book of Life, and sometime during the coming year, you will die. This is a day for judgment, atonement, and cleansing.

Now, why do they *fast*? Three times in our text, it says to "*humble your souls*" (vv. 27, 29, 32). The NIV says, "*deny yourself.*" The word for *humble (or deny)* is *anah*. Now, if you do a word study, you will find this word used in many places in the Old Testament. Let me read a few of them to you and I want you to notice what is commonly practiced as a form of *anah*.

> "Why have we **fasted** and You do not see? Why have we **humbled ourselves** (anah) and You do not notice? Behold, on the day of your fast you find your desire, And drive hard all your workers."
> Isaiah 58:3

> "Is it a **fast** like this which I choose, a day for a man to **humble himself** (anah)? Is it for bowing one's head like a reed, And for spreading out sackcloth and ashes as a bed? Will you call this a **fast**, even an acceptable day to the Lord?" Isaiah 58:5

> "Then I proclaimed a **fast** there at the river of Ahava, that we might **humble ourselves** (anah) before our God to seek from Him a safe journey for us, our little ones, and all our possessions." Ezra 8:21

> *"But as for me, when they were sick, my clothing was sackcloth; I* **humbled my soul** *(anah) with* **fasting***; And my prayer kept returning to my bosom."* Psalm 35:13

Rabbis have always taught that *fasting* must be one of the features of humbleness for Yom Kippur. It was one of five things that Jews were expected to do on this day.

1. No eating or drinking
2. No bathing or washing
3. No anointing
4. No wearing leather shoes
5. No cohabitation

The Day of Atonement was a day to lay aside thoughts of *everything* else. Worldly business was laid aside. Thoughts of satisfying the body were laid aside. It was a day to show the Lord how sorrowful you were for the sins you had committed during the past year. And it was a day that Jews were expected to be *together*. As we see in verse 26, it was a holy convocation (or assembly) and they were not to do any work. What does it sound like to you? The body of the bride is together and not working? It is Sabbath. These people would meet and discuss issues and encourage one another all day.

Now, think about something with me. Yom Kippur is the one day of the year that the high priest could go into the Holy of Holies and be in the presence of the Lord, right? What did he have to do before he went in? Could he be *unclean* and come into His presence? What happened if he wasn't clean? He died. So, it is the one day a year that man stood in the presence of God, and, depending on if he was clean or not, he either lived or died.

Do you see how Yom Kippur looks forward to the day in which we will all stand before God? If we are clean because we have accepted Jesus, we will live eternally with Him. If we are not clean because we haven't accepted Jesus, we won't. Yom Kippur looks forward to the day of judgment. Jesus teaches about this day of Judgment in Matthew 25. Jesus says that He will establish His throne and judge all the nations. He will put the sheep on His right and goats on His left. The sheep (those that followed Him and accepted Jesus) will be welcomed into His kingdom. The goats (those that always knew a better way and didn't follow Him) will be turned away and sent into the eternal fire. Could it be that this judgment will happen on the very day of Yom Kippur?

Turn to **2 Corinthians 5:9-10**. Yom Kippur is a yearly reminder that there is a judgment day. Every one of us will stand before the Lord and give an account of our life. Understand that this verse is not simply talking about the idea of simply accepting Christ and going to Heaven. It is talking about being *recompensed*. It is talking about believers getting *paid back* for things done that were **pleasing** to Him. What does that mean? Hebrews 13:21 tells us that the only thing **pleasing** to Him are things that are done in *His will.* My plea to you today is this: *Live a life in light of eternity. Listen to your Heavenly Father and obey what He tells you to do. It is **only** those things that we will be paid back for in eternity. Not "good" things that He doesn't tell us to do. LISTEN TO HIM AND OBEY!*

SUKKOT (verses 33-44)

Let's first look at some basics about Sukkot. It is also called the **Feast of Tabernacles** or the **Feast of Booths**. It is one of the three pilgrimage festivals in which God expected all males to travel to Jerusalem to celebrate (Exodus 23:14, 17). The other two are **Passover** and **Pentecost**. Sukkot is a thanksgiving festival which thanks God for the harvest of the year that lasts seven days, with the eighth day being a *holy convocation* to the Lord (v. 36). That eighth day is called the "great day of the feast". Keep that in mind. You will need to remember that later today.

The name is important for us to understand. Sukkot is the plural form of *sukkah*. A *sukkah* is a temporary dwelling or shelter. Our text says that all of Israel was to live in a *sukkah* during the seven days of Sukkot. What was the purpose of the people living in these temporary shelters during Sukkot? It was a *reminder* of how God led Israel out of Egypt, and how they dwelled in tents for 40 years in the desert. He provided everything they needed during those 40 years. He gave them water in a place where there was very little water. He gave them food (manna) in a place where there was no food. He protected their feet and their sandals didn't wear out. He provided direction with a cloud by day and pillar of fire by night. We have talked about this before. What else did the cloud and pillar of fire provide? Protection from the heat of the sun and the coolness of the night. So, while Israel is living in their tents during Sukkot, it was a time to remember God's **presence**, **protection**, and **provision**.

By the way, do you realize that Israel wasn't alone as they lived in *sukkahs* during those years? God lived in the *Tent* of Meeting. The *Sukkah* of Meeting. Neither the people of Israel nor God lived in permanent houses until they made it to the Promised Land. Remember that little nugget as well.

What did these *sukkot* look like during this festival? They were small, three-sided structures. They were made from wild branches of olive, myrtle, palm, and other leafy trees (Neh. 8:15). Their roof would be made of anything that grows from the ground (branches, bushes, etc.). They would space out the roof material so that they could see the stars...the same stars their ancestors could see as they were in their *sukkot* for forty years in the desert. Traditionally, children get involved when constructing these *sukkot* as well. After the structure is complete, kids get to decorate with fruit. They often tie them from strings and let them hang from the roof. I want you to understand how important it is for the Jews to involve their children in these events. What did the text say about Sukkot in verse 43? It was something that God wanted His people to do so that *generations* would know the history of what He did as He led them out of Egypt and was with them! As a matter of fact, it says that Sukkot is to be a **perpetual statue throughout your generations** (verse 41). It wasn't something to be done until the Messiah arrived. It wasn't something to be done until the Pentecost happened and the Holy Spirit indwelled in us. It wasn't something to be done until the Temple became destroyed. *Sukkot was designed as a forever thing.* Read **Zechariah 14:16-19**. In the end times, *all nations* will gather to celebrate Sukkot! See, Sukkot not only looks to the past about how God provided His **presence**, **protection**, and **provision**. It looks to the future to say that one day *all of us* will be **with Him**. There is a day coming when we will all be celebrating Sukkot together in the presence of our King.

You need to understand what a **joyful** time Sukkot is to Israel. The *love* Sukkot. It is their thanksgiving! But it is much more than just being thankful for what God *has* done. It is a time that looks forward to the time when God's people will be with Him for all eternity! It is a yearly reminder that there is an even *greater* joy to come.

Let's talk about this rejoicing. Look at **verse 40**. This is the only festival that rejoicing is commanded by God. You also see this found in Deuteronomy 16:14. But, there was a problem. *How* were they supposed to rejoice? God doesn't specify the exact way! If I told you to rejoice, what would you do?

Now, our text does say that they were supposed to use what Jews call the *four spices* during Sukkot. They would gather branches of palm, myrtle, and willow trees and wrap their stems together to make a "waving palm" which is called a *lulav*. The fourth thing they used was a citrus fruit called an *etrog*. Just outside one of our hotels in Israel was an *etrog* tree. So, the *lulav* and the *etrog* was supposed to be used in this rejoicing in some way. So just imagine 3 million people in Jerusalem for Sukkot. They would march around singing Psalms 113-118. When they came to Psalm 118:1 (*Give thanks to the Lord, for He is good*), they would wave their *four spices (lulav and etrog)* in the air. Again, when they came to Psalm 118:25 (*Lord, save us!*), they would wave their *four spices* in the air again.

Water Ceremony – There were two ceremonies that happened at Sukkot that you need to know about because they directly relate to when Jesus taught some massive truths about Himself. The first ceremony is the water ceremony. You must understand the timing of this festival. It happens in the late fall. There have not been any rains in 8 months. Their cisterns that hold their water are low. Springs are weak. What do you think the big prayer is at Sukkot? *God, please send rain!* When they are waving their palm branches and during Psalm 118:25 (Lord, save us!), it is because they are asking Him to save them by sending rain! Their chant was *Hoshana, Hoshana, Hoshana.* "Save us, Save us, Save us!" Make no mistake, "save us" was not "send the Messiah" in this case. They were meaning, "Send rain, God! We need you to save us because, without rain, we will die."

Here is how the water ceremony happened. Each day of the Feast of Tabernacles, the people would gather at the Pool of Siloam. A priest would fill a golden pitcher of living water from the pool as the people changed Isaiah 12:3 – "*With joy you will draw water from the wells of salvation.*" The water was carried up the hill to the Temple and they would enter through the "Water Gate." The crowds would be following behind the priest carrying their *lulav* in their right hand and their *etrog* in their left hand. As they went up to the Temple, they would sing Psalms 113-118 while waving their *lulav*. When they made it to the Temple, the priest climbed the steps of the altar and poured the water into a bowl on the altar. He, then, poured wine into another bowl on the altar. It was a beautiful ceremony full of rejoicing. As a matter of fact, one rabbi around the time of Jesus said, "*Anyone who has not seen this water ceremony has never seen rejoicing in his life.*"

On the final day of the ceremony, they added one other thing. They still got the water from the Pool of Siloam, but the priest would go around the altar seven times before pouring the water. All the while, the people would be shouting "Hoshana, Hoshana, Hoshana." As he lifted the pitcher to pour the water, the crowd became silent. It is the only time there is silence.

Listen to what John 7:37-39 says:

> *Now on the last day, the great day of the feast, Jesus stood and cried out, saying, "If anyone is thirsty, let him come to Me and drink. He who believes in Me, as the Scripture said, 'From his innermost being will flow rivers of living water.'" But this He spoke of the Spirit, whom those who believed in Him were to receive; for the Spirit was not yet given, because Jesus was not yet glorified.*

Now, the **only** time Jesus could have said this statement and people actually heard him would have been when the priest goes to pour the water on the altar. That is the only time that the crowd would have been silent, rather than rejoicing! And at that moment, Jesus says that **He** is the true source of nourishment. And if we drink from Him, we will have *rivers* of living water flowing from us. Do you get it? The people were crying out for salvation and asking God to send rain. Jesus says – I am *both*. I am your salvation. I am your water source. Come to me!

Lighting ceremony – One other ceremony that comes into play in the life of Jesus involving Sukkot. In the Court of the Woman in the Temple, there were four tall stands. They were 75 feet tall. Each had four branches at the top of the stand with a huge bowl. At Sukkot, the Mishnah says that four young men would climb ladders to the top of these 75-foot tall candle stands carrying 10-gallon pitchers of oil. You won't believe what they used for wicks. They knotted used undergarments of the priests. Specifically, the Mishnah says it was the "worn out drawers and girdles of the priests." You can't make this stuff up. Just imagine the scene of 16 lamps burning 75 feet in the air. This happened on the first day of Sukkot and would remain lit throughout the entire festival. Rabbis said that *all* Jerusalem was lit from these. It must have been spectacular to them. They didn't have any lighting after dark. One time a year, all of Jerusalem was lit.

Just after Jesus says that He is the true *living water* at the water ceremony, we get to His statements in **John 8:12**. *"I am the light of the world; he who follows Me will now walk in darkness, but will have the light of life."* Do you know where Jesus was standing when He made this statement? John 8:20 says He was in the treasury...which is located in the Court of Women. He was standing beside the huge lamps that were providing light for all of Jerusalem.

Do you know what the very next story is in the Bible? There is a man who was born blind in John 9. Jesus specifically says in the story that He is the light of the world. He spits on the ground, puts clay on the man's eyes, and tells him to wash in the Pool of Siloam. As he washed in the same pool that the priests just retrieved living water out of during Sukkot, he could see. **Water** and **light** were both evident in this miracle. We miss that because we don't understand Sukkot.

Before we finish, I want us to remember something that we talked about earlier. During Sukkot, God told Israel to build *sukkahs*, temporary dwellings, to remember their temporary dwellings as they left Egypt. Sukkot is a reminder every year to a Jew that this home is temporary. One day, we will be living in our permanent home. Are you living like you are home? Do your time, thoughts, money, and effort reflect that you are putting stock in the tent you are living in now? Or do they reflect that you are constantly longing for your true home? Put it another way – whose kingdom are you living for? This world's kingdom? Or God's Kingdom?

Was Jesus born on Sukkot? Many scholars are convinced that Jesus was born on Sukkot. Why?

- John 1:14 says, *"And the Word became flesh, and **dwelt** among us."* The Greek word here is *skēnóō* which is the Greek word for the Hebrew word *sukkah*. It means *tabernacled*. Why would John use that word? Could it be that Jesus was born on *Sukkot*?
- Luke 2:8 says that Jesus was born while the shepherds were "in the fields." There is only a 3- to 4-month window when shepherds are in the fields. The fields are where the farmers live. Shepherds only go in the fields *after* the wheat harvest and *before* the rainy season. Rains begin in early November in Israel. During my recent trip to Israel (during late September/early October), we saw at least 15 shepherds in fields. During my previous trip to Israel in May two years ago, I did not see a single shepherd in the fields.
- Luke 2:14 says that the angels sang a song to the shepherds – *"Glory to God in the highest, and on earth peace among men with whom He is pleased."* History records that Levites sang this song in the Temple during the Feast of Tabernacles.
- How much older was John the Baptist compared to Jesus? **6 months** (Luke 1:36). Zechariah was a priest in the division of Abijah. He was serving in the Temple when he was visited by Gabriel and told his wife, Elizabeth, would give birth to a son. We know from records that he

would have been serving in late June. If Elizabeth got pregnant immediately (as the Greek text implies), this would put John the Baptist's birth around Passover the following year. Six months later would be the birth of Jesus. It would fall late September or October…right at the time of Sukkot.

CONCLUSION

There are seven feasts:

1. **Passover** – Five days before Passover is lamb selection. Five days later, the lamb is killed. What happened to Jesus five days before Passover? That is the day of the Triumphal entry. Why did He come on *that* day? He was the lamb. Then, what happened on Passover? He died.
2. **Unleavened Bread** - This is when you put grain in the ground and pray for God to bring the harvest during the coming year. Their prayer is, "Give us life out of the Earth." What was happening to Jesus on this feast? While every religious Jew was praying for God to give them life out of the Earth, Jesus was being buried (planted).
3. **First Fruits** – This is when you bring the beginning of your harvest to Jerusalem and you bless God for the first part of the harvest. What happens to Jesus as First Fruits began? He rose as the first fruits of those who rise from the dead (Paul says in 1 Cor. 15:20).
4. **Shavuot/Pentecost** – This is the feast that celebrates the Ten Commandments coming down from Mt. Sinai as well as the beginning of the late harvest. What happened on Shavuot? The Holy Spirit came down. When the Ten Commandments came down, what did Moses find? Golden calf. How many people died because of it? 3000. The same day, 1300 years later, the Holy Spirit came down, how many people believed? 3000. *Do you understand that every piece of the Christian Bible falls into the framework of the Hebrew world?*
5. **Trumpets** – This is the feast that announces that the judgment day is coming. In the life of Jesus, we have seen Him enter on Lamb Selection, be killed on Passover, planted in the ground on Unleavened Bread, raised on First Fruits, send the Holy Spirit on Pentecost. What is next in His life? The 2nd coming. Wouldn't it be just like Jesus to come back on Rosh Hashanah? He hasn't missed a feast yet!
6. **Yom Kippur** – This is the judgment day.
7. **Sukkot** – This is the Promised Land feast. This is Heaven.

If Jesus was born at Sukkot, then our Messiah (the light of the world) was conceived at Hanukkah (the festival of lights). He was born as the *bread of life* in Bethlehem (which means *house of bread*) during the Feast of Tabernacles (as He tabernacle among us). The lamb of God was selected on Lamb selection Sunday and died as our perfect Lamb at Passover. He was planted in the ground at Unleavened Bread. He was raised at First Fruits. He sent the Holy Spirit at Pentecost, and He will return at the sound of the last trumpet (Feast of Trumpets).

The Great White Throne Judgement (of Revelation 20) will be at the Day of Atonement, and the Father will dwell with man at the end of the age when the Feast of Tabernacles ultimately will be fulfilled as He tabernacles with us for all eternity as it says in Revelation 21:3.

Eye for an Eye

Without any context, Leviticus 24 really seems out of place. The first nine verses deal with maintaining oil and bread in the tabernacle. The rest of the chapter deals with a case of blasphemy against the Lord. It doesn't really seem to fit with all the festivals that we spent five weeks talking about from Leviticus 23. It also doesn't seem to fit with Leviticus 25 which deals with the Sabbath year and the Year of Jubilee. I want us to walk through Leviticus 24 and we will address this issue later after we look at what is in the chapter.

Read Leviticus 24:1-4. The first instruction in Leviticus 24 is for the golden lampstand to be lit continually. This was a job of the High Priest. We talked about this back in Exodus 37. What is another name for the golden lampstand? *Menorah.* I don't want to get into another detailed lesson on the menorah today, but I want you to remember two things about it. First of all, what event did it remind Israel about? We have said that the tabernacle was to be a portable replica of Mt. Sinai, where Israel became the bride to God. What event at Sinai involved something on fire? *The burning bush.* The menorah was a continual reminder of how God showed up to Moses. But, even more important to our daily walk, we talked about the fact that Jesus tells us that **He** is the *light of the world* (John 8:12). He is our menorah that constantly burns. But He also says that **we** are the *light of the world* (Matthew 5:14-16). Just like the lampstand in the tabernacle was to burn continuously, we are to *constantly* shine for the world to see Jesus in us.

Read Leviticus 24:5-9. Not only was the High Priest to burn the menorah continuously, but he was also to make sure there were twelve loaves of bread placed on the table of showbread every Sabbath. These loaves of bread were a symbolic offering to God. Why were there twelve? It represents the twelve tribes of Israel. The only thing separating the bread from God was a curtain. These loaves of bread were a picture that the twelve tribes would be constantly devoted to God who was in their midst. Do you remember what happens in 1 Samuel 21? David and his men were hungry. David asked for five loaves of bread, but the only bread on hand was the showbread, or the Bread of the Presence. Later, Jesus refers to the story of David and his men eating this consecrated bread when Pharisees were questioning Him about picking grain and eating them on the Sabbath (Matthew 12). All of that is referring to this bread that the High Priest was to put out every Sabbath in the tabernacle.

Read Leviticus 24:10-11. In the middle of God giving all these instructions about His festivals and maintaining oil and bread in the tabernacle, we get to this story of a blasphemer. Who were this man's parents? His mother was an Israelite and his father was an Egyptian. A fight broke out with this man and someone else. What did he do during the fight? He *"blasphemed the Name. and cursed."* What did we say about the Name of God? Who could say it? *The only time it could be said was during the Day of Atonement when the High Priest was in the Holy of Holies making atonement for all of Israel.* To this day, Jews will not say the Name of God?

Why? The Ten Commandments. God says not to take His Name in vain. So, even in Scripture, we see words like "Adonai" (Lord), "Elohim" (God), and "HaShem" (the Name). After they returned from Babylonian captivity (500 BC), Jews really didn't use it at all. However, this man in Leviticus 24 blasphemed the Name. That is a serious offense.

What did Moses do? **Read Leviticus 24:12.** Moses waited on God to tell him what to do. We see Moses go to the Lord three other times in Scripture before making a decision about something. In Numbers 9, it is the second Passover. The people are in the Sinai Desert and some of them were unintentionally unclean from touching a dead body. Should they still celebrate Passover? Moses wasn't sure so He consulted God who told them to do what? *Have the unclean celebrate Passover one month later.* In Numbers 15, a man is caught gathering wood on the Sabbath. They bring him to Moses. He didn't know what to do with him. So, he waits for God to tell him. *The man was to be stoned outside of camp.* In Numbers 27, we see the question of inheritance with the daughters of Zelophehad when their father died in the wilderness. Moses isn't sure how to rule, so he consults God. God gave the daughters the land. My point is that, over and over, Moses asked God's opinion. God is a big God. He doesn't mind when you ask Him for help. As a matter of fact, He welcomes it. Don't be afraid to involve Him in your decisions but **follow Him** when He gives you an answer.

Let's look at God's response as to what He wanted them to do with the blasphemer. **Read Leviticus 24:13-16**. Any idea why the people were to lay their hands on the head of the blasphemer? In Leviticus 16, the High Priest as to lay his hands on the scapegoat on the Day of Atonement. Specifically, it says in verse 21, it was to transfer the sins to the animal. Jews teach that the people were guilty by simply *hearing* the blasphemer desecrated God's sacred Name. So, laying on their hands on him is a picture of transferring this guilt back to him. And this man was stoned. Let me ask you a question – In verses 15 and 16, we see a difference between **cursing** God and **blaspheming** Him. What is the difference? Other than the word "curses" and "blasphemes" in these verses, do you notice any other difference? Verse 15 says "his God" – *Elohim*. Verse 16 says "the name of the Lord" – *Yahweh*. Like we talked about a few moments ago. Israel *knew* they were not to take God's Holy Name lightly. If so, you are *blaspheming* His Name. The penalty in the Old Testament for that is death! Today, when Jews come to *Yahweh* in the text, they will always say "my Lord" or "the Name." They don't want to take any chances of blaspheming the Name.

For the rest of this lesson, I want to focus on this idea of punishment in the Old Testament being an "eye for an eye." **Read Leviticus 24:17-22.**

About eight years ago, I received word that one of my patients had a mother who was missing. The child was less than a year old and I had seen his mom in the office quite a few times with her son. As time passed, the truth came out. Her boyfriend's parents had killed the mother and burned her body on their property. The reason? *They didn't think she was a good mom, so they wanted to raise their grandson.* This has actually been made into a couple of different 60-minute programs like Dateline, if you are interested in that sort of thing.

For years, I have always considered the idea of an "eye for an eye" to be pretty harsh. But think about it...when we read about the punishment of an "eye for an eye," God is teaching about *proportional retribution.* You see, God says that **punishment should fit the crime**. The punishment should not be *harsher* or *weaker* than the crime committed.

Understand the culture of the time period. Let's say a man killed another man in 1300 BC. We know from ancient sources that there was the possibility of the death penalty. However, what happened in most cases is that the one committing the murder could pay money and it would take place of the death penalty. This would be an example of the punishment *not* fitting the crime. The punishment is **weaker** than the crime. God was not interested in having a weak punishment system. So, He made it clear in verse 17 – "*If a man takes the life of any human being, he shall **surely** be put to death.*"

The punishment should also not be **harsher** than the crime. For instance, if a man gouges out the eye of the second man, it is not okay for the second man to gouge out the first man's eye *and* cut off an ear. This idea of "eye for an eye" was a way to put limits on punishments. It is a system that makes sure that the rich and poor were treated equally when it came to punishment. A rich person couldn't pay money to get out of penalties and a poor person could not be taken advantage of by going above and beyond in punishment.

Did you know we see the teaching of an "eye for an eye" three times in the Old Testament? Not only do we see it in Leviticus 24, but we also see it in **Exodus 21:22-25** and **Deuteronomy 19:18-21**. Here is the kicker about the instruction of an "eye for an eye." All three times, the issue was **not** about how to respond *individually* when someone wronged a person. An "eye for an eye" was a guideline for the *judge* in the situation.

So, what about the individual who was wronged? Listen to the words of Jesus:

> "*You have heard that it was said, '**AN EYE FOR AN EYE, AND A TOOTH FOR A TOOTH.**' But I say to you, do **not** resist an evil person; but whoever slaps you on your right cheek, turn the **other** to him also. If anyone wants to sue you and take your shirt, let him have your **coat also**. Whoever forces you to go one mile, go with him **two**. Give to him who asks of you, and do **not** turn away from him who wants to borrow from you.*" Matthew 5:38-42

When someone *wrongs* us, we must be mindful that our role is not to be judge and jury. **God** is the One and only Judge (James 4:12). Jesus teaches that our role is to display *grace* to this world. Almost daily, I hear someone in my office talk about karma. Karma is the exact opposite of grace. Karma is someone getting what they deserve. Grace is someone getting what they *don't* deserve. In my flesh, it is easy for me to wish karma on those around me. Especially when someone is being rude. Believe me, it happens all the time in my office. But **grace** is what points them to Jesus. Why? John 1:14 says, *"And the Word became flesh, and dwelt among us, and we saw His glory, glory as of the only begotten from the Father, full of grace and truth."* You are never more like Jesus than when you are dispensing grace to the unworthy.

Know dispensing this kind of *grace* to those around us only comes from Him. It is not a natural thing to give grace. Actually, it is *impossible* without the very life of Jesus living within us and being allowed to display that grace through us. We must be sensitive to the Holy Spirit in this. Our flesh will absolutely war with giving grace in these situations. But if we want others to see Jesus in us, *grace* will be one of the hallmarks of our lives.

∎∎

NOTE: Grace does *not* mean giving sin a "free pass." That is not what Jesus came to do. A free pass says, "Friend, I see your sin. I am not going to call it what it is. I am going to ignore it." That is *not* love. How does God see this? Well, He says, "I see your sin. I name your sin specifically to you through the conviction of the Holy Spirit. I have made a way for your specific sin to be dealt with at the cross of Christ. You don't have to try to ignore it or cover it or deal with it on your own. Because of Christ, you have a way to be free from your sin. Confess it and repent, and you will be forgiven. I will help you change."

Grace calls out sin because of love. Grace lives out Galatians 6:1-2:

> *Brethren, even if anyone is caught in any trespass, you who are spiritual, restore such a one in a spirit of gentleness; each one looking to yourself, so that you too will not be tempted. Bear one another's burdens, and thereby fulfill the law of Christ.*

A grace-giver is not simply a doormat that accepts everything around us. A grace-giver sees sin the way God sees it and looks for ways to bring others to Christ in those shortcomings.

∎∎

Let's come back to the question of *why* God placed the events Leviticus 24 in the middle of His instructions on festivals. It seems so out-of-place. What did the first 9 verses address? Giving God continuous worship through the menorah constantly burning and fresh showbread weekly. The festivals are observed *once a year*. God is reminding His people that they are not to be festival-only believers. They were to *continually* worship Him. Just like we are not to be Sunday-only Christians. We are to *continually* worship Him.

What about this story of the blasphemer? God's Word is a real story. It is pretty simple, really. As God was giving His instructions, this event happened. So, God pauses His instructions and deals with this issue. If you were making it up, you wouldn't put this story here. But that is how it happened. Be confident that God's Word is not fiction.

Action points:

- Like the menorah, *continually* shine your light to the world.
- Like Moses, consult the Lord when making a decision.
- Like Jesus, give grace to the undeserving.

Ready to Help Family

We are getting close to the end of our journey through Leviticus together. Today, we are in Leviticus 25. There is a lot for us to get into today, so let's just begin by reading **Leviticus 25:1-7**.

This section addresses the idea of a **sabbath year for the land**. This isn't the first time it is mentioned in Scripture. Turn back to **Exodus 23:10-12**. Once a week, God wanted His people to stop working in their fields and rest. Much like He rested on the seventh day (Genesis 2:2). The seventh day of the week has always been set aside *for* God. We have talked about this in great detail previously. But, understand that He also said that every *seventh year* was also to be set aside for Himself. So, weekly, the people were supposed to stop working the ground and rest. Let me be very clear. **Rest** does *not* have the idea of **relaxation** as its focus. Instead, it is a time to step back from our work and recognize that God is the One who provides for and satisfies our needs. It has nothing to do with what we bring to the table. A day of rest is a day of worship because we realize our total dependence on Him.

Let's think about this sabbath year for a moment. For six years, the Israelite was to work in his field. We have talked about the *nahala* which is the land given to the family units in Israel. You can still see these today. A family was to work that field (usually ½ acre to an acre in size) for six years. On the seventh, God says that the fields should have a "sabbath rest" (Lev. 25:4) and "lie fallow" (Ex. 23:10). What is the *purpose* of the sabbath year according to Exodus 23:11-12? Two things – it was for the *needy* so they could eat, and it was for the *animals and slaves* to have rest.

There is something else about this sabbath year. Deuteronomy 31:10-13 tells us that something special was supposed to happen during the Feast of Booths celebration during the sabbath year. The Law was to be read to the entire nation. Now, just because God gave His people a command to do observe this sabbath year, does that mean that His people always practiced it? No. In 2 Chronicles 36:21, we find that Israel neglected this sabbath year command. Do you know what their punishment was? The land had to lay desolate for **70** years. We call it the Babylonian captivity. God says it was because His people were not observing His commandment of the sabbath year.

Do you think the people started observing sabbath year when they came back? You better believe it! Nehemiah 8 talks about all the people gathering and listening to the law of Moses on the first day of the seventh month. Do you remember the story? They had just returned from exile and Ezra begins to read the law and the people begin to weep. They get to the part of God telling them to build tabernacles (or booths) during the seventh month. So, what did they do? They went out and collected materials to make booths. It was immediate obedience. In chapter 10 of Nehemiah, we see that they begin to observe the sabbath year. And that is exactly what happened. Even in the period of time between the Old and New Testaments, we see historical records showing that Israel was obeying the sabbath year. So, this is the first part of Leviticus 25. God wanted His people to have a year in which the land was totally devoted to Him since it belonged to Him to begin with. He wanted that year to be a time of focusing on the needy and giving rest to the slaves doing the work.

The next section of Leviticus 25 deals with the **Year of Jubilee**. The land was to lie fallow every seven years, but after the *seventh* sabbatical year, the fiftieth year, there was a Year of Jubilee. This is a time that each person was to return to his personal property. Now, the Year of Jubilee began on one of the feasts. Which one? The Day of Atonement (v. 9). Read **verse 10**. The Year of Jubilee proclaimed "release" to the inhabitants. Another translation says it proclaimed "liberty." This is a big deal. To understand this, we need to understand a little more about the culture.

If a person has a debt, what can he do to pay it off? Well, if he doesn't have money, he can offer two things. The first is his *nahala*. The second is himself. So many Jews became *enslaved* to other Jews because they had debts that they could not pay. Every fiftieth year, two things happened. Their *nahala* return to them and they were set free. Do you remember the slave laws we talked about in Exodus 21? A slave was to serve his master for six years and, in the seventh year, he had a choice. He could go free or he could willingly submit to the master because he loved them. In that case, he would have his ear pierced with an awl on the doorpost. Even those slaves that were said to permanently been a slave of their master were released on the Year of Jubilee. It was a year where everything was supposed to be returned back to the rightful owners. Also, understand that it truly protected the weak. The rich couldn't just buy up everything they wanted and have it passed down to their families forever.

We read in verse 12 that the people were to eat crops out of their fields. Question – when were those crops planted? This was the *third* year of those crops producing fruit. This would be crops planted in the fall two years prior. They already fed the family during that spring and summer. The following year would have been a sabbath year. Could they plant crops? No. They relied on the previous year. And then God says not to plant crops during the Year of Jubilee. Do you understand that this was a test of their *faith*? God has told them over and over that He would take care of them. Then, He tells them to do something that doesn't make sense. *Don't plant for two consecutive seasons.* Will they trust Him totally and do what He says, even when it doesn't make sense? They can't go to the grocery store for food. This is their life that is on the line. They better *know* that He will provide.

Our text continues in verses 13-17 by talking about how the purchase price would be adjusted based on the years remaining until the Year of Jubilee. That makes sense. If I only have one year to use your land, I should be a smaller price than if I have forty years to use it.

Verses 18-22 return to this idea of *how will God provide during the sabbath year and the Year of Jubilee*? Simply, He just wanted them to obey Him and trust Him. It was a time for Israel to realize that **God** is the provider of all. Their crops did not depend on the labor *they* provided. He was the sustainer. Listen, we have to understand that God wants us to work hard. He wants us to use our energy, talents, and gifts that He has given us. He wants us to not be lazy. But, at the end of the day, He wants us to know that our needs are met by *Him*, not by what *we* bring to the table. This sabbath year and this Year of Jubilee was a regular reminder that He is the ultimate provider and sustainer.

The next section of Leviticus 25 (verses 23-38) focus on the redemption of property. I want us to focus on **verses 25-28**. There were three possible outcomes if an Israelite sold his property to another Israelite:

1. It could be recovered by a **kinsman redeemer**.
2. It could be bought back by the **seller** himself.
3. It would be returned in the year of Jubilee.

I want to focus on the first possible outcome. If someone sold his *nahala*, the nearest relative (*gṓēl*) had the obligation to buy back or redeem (*gā́al*) the land. This **kinsman redeemer** had two jobs in this: *reclaim the land* and *restore the relative*. According to the Bible, who was Israel's kinsman redeemer? God. Isaiah 63:16 says, "*You, O LORD, are our Father, Our Redeemer (gā́al) from of old is Your name.*" **Isaiah 54:5-8**. God is the **kinsman redeemer**. He comes to *reclaim* and *restore* that which are His.

I would argue that He wants to use *us* as His hands and feet in doing the same thing today. We have so many around us that need to know our kinsman redeemer. They need to know that He wants to *reclaim* them for His purposes. They need to know that He has a mission for them, and He wants to *restore* them to that mission. Now, let's make this personal. Our church here should have the same mission. We *are* His Body. If that is the case, we should be the kinsman redeemers of our communities. But, let's just start with this church family. We all know people who should be here today. We know people that used to be a part of our family and, for some reason, are no longer here. It is not that they have moved membership to another church. They just aren't here. Do you realize that our job is to get them back into the family? We are to go to them. We are not to have an attitude of, "Well, if they want to be a part of us, they will come on back." No! We have an enemy that is deceiving them into believing that it is possible to be a lone-ranger Christian. But God wants each of us to be plugged into a body so that we can be sharpened by one another and use our gifts that He has entrusted to us! However, there is another side of the equation of this kinsman redeemer. It is not good enough just to get someone back in the fold. A kinsman redeemer's job is to make sure that they are *restored*. Meaning that these people don't just sit on the sidelines and watch for years before they have a job to do. Restoration means that they are equipped to be fully functioning part of the body. When someone comes

117

in, we are to be a body that looks at their gifts and finds a way for them to be utilized.

I feel like there needs to be some redeeming happening right now in our church body. I feel like there are people that need to be sought after, brought back in, and restored. Will you be God's hands and feet in this restoration? Will you be His mouthpiece to someone today or this week?

I want to finish today by looking at one more verse in this chapter.

If any of your fellow Israelites become poor and are unable to support themselves among you, help them as you would a foreigner and stranger, so they can continue to live among you.
Leviticus 25:35 (NIV)

From December 2007 until June 2009, the United States was in a terrible recession. An incredible **73%** of people in the United States either lost their job or had a close family member or friend lose their job. I remember the intense anxiety that many were feeling. But I also remember the countless stories of **family members** stepping up and *helping* those in need. Why did they do it? Well, they were *family*.

In Leviticus 25, the Lord gives instructions to help **fellow Israelites** if they became poor. Wait a minute, *fellow Israelites*? Like, *any* of them? Or just the ones that are related? **The call was for *any* Israelite to be taken care of by fellow Israelites if they became poor because they *were* family!** These people were God's chosen people. He was their father. They were His sons. So, even if they weren't related by blood, they *were* family.

Today, **believers in Jesus Christ** are His children. *I am a **His son!***

> *For you have not received a spirit of slavery leading to fear again, but you have received a spirit of **adoption as sons** by which we cry out, "**Abba! Father!**" Romans 8:15*

As I glance at the Church, I see the faces of my *brothers* and *sisters*. Sure, we don't share common DNA, but we do share the same Heavenly Father. As I look at those people, the Lord calls me to **help them** if they are struggling. The Hebrew word used for *help* in Leviticus 25 (*āza*) means *to show strength that does not yield or quit*. For the believers who God has placed in my path, my command is to offer support, when needed, for as long as needed. Understand that I am not saying we are to give a blank check to any Christian asking for a hand-out. But, at the same time, I am convinced that the Church can often be selfish with our resources when there are needs within our own *family*.

Why did God instruct His people to help the poor among them? *So that those hurting Israelites could **live** among them*. This is such an important word. The word *live* used in this verse is the Hebrew word *ayah* which means *to **infuse life***. The reason God wants His people to *help* the poor within the Church is so that His Body will be **strong,** and **life will be infused** for His glory! If the Body of Christ is hurting around us, they will not have the resources to complete the ministry that God has set before them. *Who are those that God is calling me to **help** in order that they may **infuse life** for His glory?*

You know, the early church got a lot of things wrong. Look at the New Testament letters to these churches. They were baby Christians that messed up *a lot.* But, do you know one thing they got right? The idea that *their stuff* was not really *their stuff*...**everything** belongs to God! *"They sold property and possessions to **give** to **anyone who had need.**" Acts 2:45 (NIV).* Am I living life with an open hand, ready to meet the needs of my family in Christ that God has placed around me? Or do I think that *my* possessions are *my* possessions? Is my life *really* all about Him?

One last thing. Do you remember that we said it proclaimed "release" or "liberty" to the inhabitants? It is the Hebrew word *deror*. Isaiah 61:1-3 says that the Messiah will come to proclaim *deror* to the captives. It is exactly what Jesus quotes at the beginning of His ministry in Luke 4:18-19. He came to proclaim *derar*. He came to **remove our debt** and **restore us to our proper place**.

CliffsNotes

You shall not make for yourselves idols, nor shall you set up for yourselves an image or a sacred pillar, nor shall you place a figured stone in your land to bow down to it; for I am the LORD your God. You shall keep My sabbaths and reverence My sanctuary; I am the LORD.
Leviticus 26:1-2

In high school, reading was definitely not a hobby of mine. My attitude was this: give me some type of ball and point me to some type of court, but don't give me a book! Because of this, I always *hated* when my name was called to read a book out loud during class. I was not a fast reader. This fact came back to haunt me when taking my ACT...a test geared for fast readers!

Just like every other school, at McKenzie High School we were required to read several novels during English class. My strategy was simple...I will skim the novel, read the CliffsNotes, and spend most of my time outdoors! *Here* is a CliffNotes copy of *To Kill a Mockingbird*. It gives the overall storyline, the list of characters, breaks down each chapter with a summary and commentary, and analysis of each character. CliffNotes is a much quicker read than the full book of *To Kill a Mockingbird* and gives you the essential information that is needed to understand the book.

As we reach Leviticus 26, the first two verses are essentially the CliffsNotes of the Mosaic covenant. Do you want to hear what is in Exodus 19-24 in a nutshell? Leviticus 26:1-2 gives you the highlights. This is so important because these two verses hold the key to what God views as the **most important points** about His covenant with Moses and His people. There are three main things:

1. **God does not want His people having idols.**

    Over and over in Scripture, God makes it clear...He wants our undivided adoration and praise. As our Creator, He deserves **all** of it. Idols take over God's rightful place in our lives. He knows that and so He tells His people to *watch for* idols and *remove* them.

    Now, in the text, He says that the people were not to set up for themselves two things: *an image* or *a sacred pillar*. I don't know if you realize just how adamant Jews were at the time of Jesus and before to steer clear from *images*. When they built their synagogues, they would have no part of any artwork that would be an image. Today, one way you can figure out when a synagogue was built is by looking for images. If they have an image of a bird or another animal, it is probably a later synagogue. Why? God didn't want His people worshipping anything *created*, He wanted them worshipping the Creator.

The people were also not to put up *sacred pillars*. This is talking about a *standing stone*. Long before the Israelites arrived in Israel, pagans in the Middle East erected sacred *standing stones* to their gods. If one of their gods had done something really important (like help win a war, helped in a famine or drought) a stone was erected as a testimony to the action of their god. It was to tell others that the god of that town did something amazing. God knew the culture of the land. So, there are times in Scripture when God told Israel to put up *standing stones* when He acted. Why? The people *knew* what standing stones were. If the Israelites set these up, they would be asked, *"What happened here?"* And it would be a chance to provide a testimony of the One true God.

I witnessed several of these stones at Gezer two years ago. They were *huge*. They were about twenty feet tall, but they also go into the ground another twenty feet. They weighed 25 tons and they came from a quarry over three miles away! That is pretty amazing considering they were put there before 3000 BC.

What events can you think of that *standing stones* were placed in the Bible?

- Jacob set up *stone pillars* at Bethel in order to remember his powerful dream, in which God reaffirmed His covenant with him (Genesis 28:18-21, 35:14-15).
- Moses built twelve *standing stones* at the foot of Mount Sinai after receiving the Ten Commandments and other laws (Exodus 24:2-4).
- The Israelites erected *standing stones* to remember their miraculous crossing of the Jordan River (Joshua 4:2-3, 8-9).
- Joshua built a *standing stone* when the covenant was renewed at Shechem (Joshua 24:27).

I want you to understand that Israel used standing stones for certain occasions. However, the standing stones were *never* to be the object of worship! Our text in Leviticus 26 says that Israel was not to set up for themselves a sacred stone **to bow down before it**. We read in Deuteronomy 16:22, *"You shall not set up for yourself a sacred pillar which the LORD your God hates."* Why would He hate the standing stones? Are they not just marking a location in which He acted? Well, I think it is because He wanted Israel to be *different*. Canaanites set up sacred stones all the time. They are all over Israel today. And they can become an object of worship. So, God wanted His people to worship *Him* rather than a stone. However, there were times, such as when Israel crossed the Jordan in Joshua 4, in which He commanded the people to put up standing stones for the purpose of their children and the generations to follow. *Do you understand why it is* **so important** *for us to be actively listening for His voice?* You can't bank on yesterday's obedience. He doesn't always want us doing the same thing over and over just because He instructed us to do something on one specific occasion. As a church, we must always be listening to His current instructions. As a people, we must be getting our orders fresh every day!

2. **God wants His people to keep the Sabbath.**

As God gave His people the CliffsNotes version of the Mosaic covenant, He makes a point of talking about the importance of the Sabbath. Have you noticed a trend as we have gone through Leviticus? How many times have we talked about the Sabbath? On one hand, I almost feel like I should apologize for teaching about the same thing over and over. However, I am only teaching about it over and over because God is talking about it over and over. Do you think it is important to Him?

I have absolutely seen the Sabbath in a different light after going through all of His instructions in Leviticus. We said last week that the Sabbath should be a day of *rest*, but there is not a hint in the Hebrew of it being a day of *relaxation*. It is a day set aside **for** God. It is our date day with our husband. Last week, we also talked about it as being a day of trust. Why? God wants us to set aside one day to not work and realize that **He** is the true provider and sustainer. Our pride wants to kick in and say, "No, I am the one working. I am the one making money for my family." God is the one who gives you the strength to do it. God is the one who gave you the job. Without His direction and power, you wouldn't be providing anything. He is providing it through you. So, Sabbath is a time to stop our work and *trust* Him to provide for us and sustain us.

3. **God wants His people to revere His sanctuary.**

The last point in the CliffNotes version of the Mosaic covenant involved His house. This is not an instruction for us to exalt our church building. As a matter of fact, He specifically tells us in His Word that **He does not live in buildings made by human hands** (Acts 7:48). So where is His sanctuary? What are we to *revere*? **Our bodies are now His temple** (1 Corinthians 6:19). He dwells within *us*. While I fall so short of *revering His sanctuary*, He calls me to *take care of His residence*.

Am I **physically** *revering His sanctuary?* This takes so much discipline and I mess this up all the time! What we are putting into our body matters. Others should know that we are under the control of Jesus based on what we put into it. Recently, our pastor, Bro. Bert, preached an entire sermon based on *self-control.* According to Galatians 5:23, self-control is part of the fruit of the Spirit. It is not easy because our flesh wars against this. Are you putting things in your body that *honor* Jesus because it is where He lives? Or are you just putting stuff in there that makes you feel good but is killing His temple?

What about exercise? We all know that exercise is so important to our health. In order to physically revere God's sanctuary, we must be active. That isn't always easy when it is forty degrees. That isn't always easy when we have a lot going on. That isn't always easy when we have an enemy telling us to sleep in and get a little more rest. Know that God wants you to view your body the way He views your body. It is His home. Do your absolute best to keep it healthy for Him.

Am I **spiritually** *revering His sanctuary?* Even more importantly from what you are physically putting into your body is what you are spiritually putting into your body. Are you **feasting** on God's Word? Don't rely on just a short devotion every morning. Devotionals are not bad, but they are someone's opinion on what God has said in His Word. Open His Word. It should be your main source of nourishment.

For the remainder of the chapter, God promised **blessings** for obedience and **penalties** for disobedience to these three instructions.

Listen to the **blessings** He promised *if* they obeyed (vv. 3-13): *Rains, fruit, security, peace, power over their enemies, children,* and *abundant food.* Look at **verses 11-13**. This is the absolute pinnacle of obedience. He promised a special relationship with Him. He would be with them. He would be their God. He would remove their burdens. Obedience meant that God would be with them and meet their needs. Right? What does Jesus talk about in Matthew 6? *Don't worry about what you will eat or what you will drink. Don't worry about what you will wear. Doesn't God care for the birds of the air and the lilies of the field? Instead, seek first His kingdom and His righteousness, and all these things will be added to you.* We have discussed this before. **Kingdom** is where the king is kinging. Jesus is telling us to *do His will*! Is His will for us to make idols? No. Is His will for us to keep the Sabbath? Yes. Is His will for us to take care of His sanctuary? Yes. Jesus is essentially restating Leviticus 26 in Matthew 6. If you **obey** the Lord and trust Him, God will meet your needs!

But what happens if Israel did not obey according to Leviticus 26?

There were **penalties** for disobedience according to verse 14-39. Do you realize this section is about three times as long as the blessings section? Now, I want you to realize something. God's heart was not really to **punish** Israel if they were disobedient. These penalties are designed to be a form of *discipline* so that they would get back on His path! God is truly full of grace and mercy. He repeatedly gives His people second chances in Scripture. He doesn't give up on us the moment we mess up. So, he uses a series of penalties that increase in severity as He tries to bring them back to Himself. He just wants them to *repent*.

First attempt (vv. 16-17) – Fear, diseases, and enemies overtaking their food.
Second attempt (vv. 18-20) – No rain and the ground will become hard.
Third attempt (vv. 21-22) – Multiply afflictions seven times and send wild beasts to destroy their children, cattle, and make them few in number.
Fourth attempt (vv. 23-26) – Look at verse 23. Why would they still act with *hostility* after all of these things? Well, the word really means *uncaring* or *indifferent*. Biblically, if you don't care or act indifferent to what God's will is, you are **hostile** towards Him. In this fourth attempt to bring them to repentance, He would bring enemies in with a sword. He would bring pestilence.
Fifth attempt (vv. 27-33) – Cannibalism because of dire famine. Utter destruction.

If you were an Israelite and heard what was at stake, wouldn't you do everything in your power to remove idols, keep the Sabbath, and revere His sanctuary? Think about this...if they *failed* the CliffsNotes test of the essentials to the Mosaic covenant, what chance did they have of *passing* the rest of His test?

God's call to them is found in verses 40-46. He wanted them to realize they were wrong. He wanted them to confess that they were not on the right path. He wanted them to turn back to Himself with their entire being. If they did this, He would remember His covenant with their ancestors. They would return to the *blessings* that He had promised. And He would be their God.

The same is true today! Let's go back to the CliffNotes of what God has on His heart. Guys, we can't get this wrong. They are too important to the Lord? *Are you serious about looking for idols and removing anything that diverts your attention from Him? Are you serious about keeping His Sabbath and making sure it is truly **His** day? Are you serious about taking care of His sanctuary?* If any of the answers to these questions is no, realize you are wrong. Confess it to Him. Get back on His path. And He will forgive you and use you as His instrument.

An Indian Giver

The last chapter of Leviticus deals with vows and dedications made to the Lord. Leviticus 1-7 discusses sacrificial offerings to the Lord. The vows and dedications of Leviticus 27 are above and beyond the sacrificial offerings earlier in the book. The vows we will be discussing as we begin this chapter were *not* mandatory. They were personal vows that express a willing devotion and the money from these vows was specifically used in the upkeep of the sanctuary.   Read **Deuteronomy 23:21-23**. We see in verse 22 that vows were *voluntary*. However, if a person vows to God, it better be kept.

This chapter is broken up into several sections based on the type of vows. The first section deals with *human vows* (verses 2-8). The second section deals with *animal vows* (verses 9-13). The third section deals with vows of *inanimate objects* (verse 14-25).

Human Vows (verses 2-8): Read **verses 2-4**. *Why* would a person want to dedicate themselves or their children in this way? Without knowing the culture, we can probably come up with some pretty good guesses. However, records of the ancient Near East are filled with these types of vows. In Mesopotamia, we read of a queen whose son was extremely sick. She vowed to the god she worshipped that *if* he recovered, she would set him apart for her god. These vows that we are discussing almost always had a *reason* for which they were given. The two reasons Israel would vow themselves or their children to God were: (1) hope of a future blessing from the Lord or (2) in fulfillment of a promise to present an offering after God gave his favor in a situation. Let me give you a few examples of where we see these vows in Scripture. In Genesis 28:20-22, Jacob has his famous dream. Do you remember what he does when he wakes up from that dream? He makes a vow. *If* God will go with him, give him food to eat, give him clothes to wear, and allow him to return to his father's house in safety, then the Lord would be his God. In Numbers 21, Israel makes a vow to God when they were going against a Canaanite king. *"If* you deliver us..." Or how about Jephthah's vow in Judges 11? *If* you will deliver me from the sons of Ammon, God, I will offer You whoever runs out of my house when I get home as a burnt offering. God delivers the sons of Ammon. When he gets home, his daughter runs out to greet him. His one and only child. And he must sacrifice her because of the vow he made to God.

We see many examples in Scripture where *vows* were given to God as a dedication *if* He acted. It was a common practice in the culture to other gods as well. But there was a difference with Israel in this vow in relation to the other cultures. Who was able to provide service at the Tabernacle? Levites. A normal person couldn't just come to the Tabernacle one day and say, "I'm here to work for God. I made Him a vow, so show me how to do all those offerings so I can work for Him." Instead, God set values for individuals that could be given to the sanctuary and would support the upkeep of it. The price set was really determined by the person's size and strength. A male between twenty and sixty would be *fifty shekels*. A female between one month and five years would be *three shekels*.

Understand how expensive this was. At this time, the wage of a worker was **one shekel** per month. Fifty shekels would be **four years** of wages. Can you imagine taking every dime you have earned over the past four years and bringing it up here for the upkeep of the church? That is what we are talking about here. These are serious vows. In addition, there is a great chance that this type of vow also involved the person taking the Nazirite vow of Numbers 6. There were people that were so moved by how God had acted in their life that they made this vow to him for themselves or their children. Think Hannah's dedication of Samuel.

Listen, I don't think God is asking any of us to give up the past four years of our income in the offering plate the next time we go to church. But, would you be willing to do something like that if He asked you to?

Animal Vows (verses 9-13): Read **verses 9 and 10**. A person could offer a cow, sheep, or goat to God. This is how the book of Leviticus begins: "*Then the LORD called to Moses and spoke to him from the tent of meeting, saying, Speak to the sons of Israel and say to them, 'When any man of you brings an offering to the LORD, you shall bring your offering of animals from the herd or the flock.'*" The book is coming full circle. As we get to Leviticus 27, we read the process of a person bringing this animal to the Lord. The text says that the animal becomes **holy**. It is set apart and must not be exchanged for a different animal. Imagine going through a hard time and saying, "God, if you just get me through this, I will give you my next born lamb." Then the lamb is born, and you think, "Yeah, but this other lamb isn't as valuable. Maybe I will give that one instead. Who will know the difference?" Or, what if you make a vow to the Lord like Jephthah. And your one and only daughter is the one that comes out to greet you. If we make a vow to the Lord, He wants us to follow through with *exactly* what we promised to give Him. He is not interested in secondary substitutes that don't cost us as much as we promised Him. We will come back to this thought in a few minutes.

Vows of Inanimate Objects (verses 14-25): These verses talk about people dedicating their house, their family land (*nahala*), or field they have purchases that were not part of the family land to the Lord. We aren't going to get into this specifically but know that this is another option when making dedications to the sanctuary.

> *Nevertheless, anything which a man sets apart to the LORD out of all that he has, of man or animal or of the fields of his own property, shall not be sold or redeemed. Anything devoted to destruction is most holy to the LORD.*
> **Leviticus 27:28**

Living in Lewis County, it is good to know a little history of Meriwether Lewis of Lewis and Clark. During their expedition, these two men documented their dealings with Native Americans in regard to gift-giving. The Native Americans had a custom of exchanging gifts with one another. If one group gave a gift, the recipient was *expected* to give a gift of the same value in return. But, one of the parties could decide they wanted their gift back in the future and reverse the trade.

In Leviticus 27, God warns His people about being Indian givers. If they set aside something for the Lord, they were **not** to take it back for personal gain! They were not to **sell it** or **redeem it**. Once they gave it to Him, their laws said they could *never* even touch it again! *It didn't really belong to them at that point.* There is a Hebrew word repeated **five times** in verses 28 and 29. It is the word *herem*. Let me read you these two verses translated from the Hebrew:

> Nevertheless, no ***herem*** (devoted thing), that a man shall ***herem*** unto Hashem of all that he has, both of man and animal, and of the fields of his possession, shall be sold or redeemed; every ***herem*** is *kodesh kodashim* (most holy) unto Hashem. No ***herem***, which shall be ***herem*** of men, shall be redeemed; but shall surely be put to death.

What is *herem*? Well, it is a word used for two things: (1) Something to be destroyed and (2) Something reserved for exclusive use in the sanctuary. In God's mind, when someone devotes something to Him (*herem*), it has exactly one purpose. It is something that becomes **most holy** to Him and that is essentially *destroyed* to us.

Let's make this personal. How many things in *my life* have been **set apart for Him**, only for *me* to snatch it back from His grasp for selfish purposes?

*Sabbath - I **know** His heart is for me to **rest** on the Sabbath. He has set aside that day to be **holy** and **His**. How often do I do **anything but rest**? How often do I take away the time designated for Him to spend on my selfish desires?*

Giving - There have been times when God has burdened my heart to set aside money for a specific purpose. What happens when life gets in the way and expenses arise? Do I shift that designated money to cover my daily needs? Or do I trust Him? This chapter ends by discussing tithing. While there are many earlier texts on tithing (all the way back to Genesis 14), this is the first time that God introduces it into law for His people. There will be future lessons on tithing as we get to other texts, but withholding tithes is robbing God according to Malachi 3:8. That is how He views it. Am I being faithful in my giving?

Prayer time - I know my Heavenly Father loves hearing my voice. That is a sacred time. But what happens when I am tired or busy? Is praying really a priority? Or do I take back time set aside for prayer to rest or catch up on work?

Bible study time - What a sweet time He gives me in His Word. That is time that is devoted to the Lord. Unfortunately, there have been far too many days in my life that I have snatched away that holy time to use it on personal gain.

Can I confess something to you? I have often been an **Indian giver** when it comes to Jesus. Far too often, I have *touched* what *rightfully belonged to Him*. Far too often, I have abused that which He sets aside as *holy* for *personal gain*. It is time that I **completely** die to *myself* and *my desires* and allow Him to remove my Indian giving ways. Will you join me in this?